As one of the world's longest established
and best-known travel brands,
Thomas Cook are the experts in travel.

For more than 135 years our
guidebooks have unlocked the secrets
of destinations around the world,
sharing with travellers a wealth of
experience and a passion for travel.

**Rely on Thomas Cook as your
travelling companion on your next trip
and benefit from our unique heritage.**

as Cook **pocket** guides

LANZAROTE

Thomas
Cook

Written by Andrew Sanger; updated by Joe Cawley

Published by Thomas Cook Publishing
A division of Thomas Cook Tour Operations Limited
Company registration no. 3772199 England
The Thomas Cook Business Park, Unit 9, Coningsby Road,
Peterborough PE3 8SB, United Kingdom
Email: books@thomascook.com, Tel: + 44 (0)1733 416477
www.thomascookpublishing.com

Produced by Cambridge Publishing Management Limited
Burr Elm Court, Main Street, Caldecote CB23 7NU

ISBN: 978-1-84848-268-5

First edition © 2006 Thomas Cook Publishing
This third edition © 2010 Thomas Cook Publishing
Text © Thomas Cook Publishing
Maps © Thomas Cook Publishing/PCGraphics (UK) Limited

Series Editor: Adam Royal
Production/DTP: Steven Collins

Printed and bound in Spain by GraphyCems

Cover photography © Thomas Cook

CONTENTS

WHAT'S IN YOUR GUIDEBOOK?

Independent authors Impartial, up-to-date information from our travel experts who meticulously source local knowledge.

Experience Thomas Cook's 165 years in the travel industry and guidebook publishing enriches every word with expertise you can trust.

Travel know-how Thomas Cook has thousands of staff working around the globe, all living and breathing travel.

Editors Travel-publishing professionals, pulling everything together to craft a perfect blend of words, pictures, maps and design.

You, the traveller We deliver a practical, no-nonsense approach to information, geared to how you really use it.

A secluded beach at Papagayo

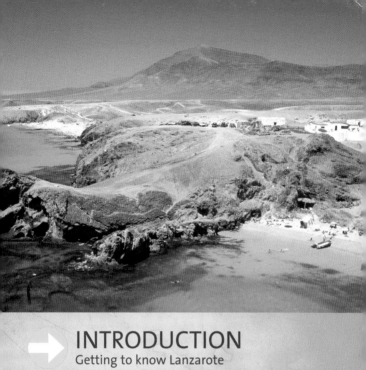

INTRODUCTION
Getting to know Lanzarote

Lanzarote

0   3 miles
0   6 km

N

City
Large Town
Small Town
Motorway
Main Road
Minor Road
Airport
POI
National Park
Boundary

Alegranza

Isla de la Graciosa
Baja del Coral

Caleta del Sebo
Mirador del Río

Punta Gorda
Playa Lambra

Pedro Barba
Punta de Pedro Barba
Playa de la Cantería

Orzola

La Caleta
Cueva de
los Verdes
Jameos
del Agua
Caleta del Campo

Yé

Guinate
Punta
Mujeres
Máguez
Arrieta

Haría

Tabayesco

Mala

Punta Pasito
Playa del Seiïjo
Charco
del Palo

Punta Ganada

Playa de
Famara

Los Valles

Famara

Teguise

Soo

Atlantic Ocean

Club La Santa

La Santa

El Cuchillo

Punta de los Cuchillos

Playa del Islote

6

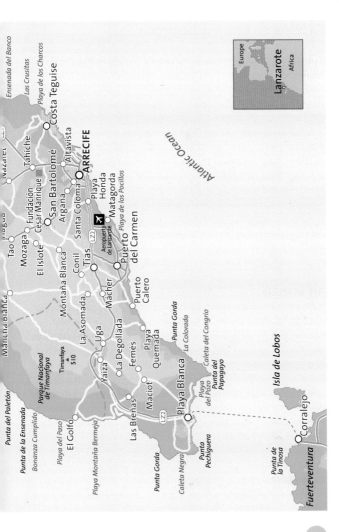

Getting to know Lanzarote

If visitors to Lanzarote come looking only for sun, sea and sand, they will not be disappointed. This most easterly and most northerly of the Canaries is the sunniest and driest of the islands, and its beaches are among the best, with pale sand that in ages past was blown over from Saharan Africa, just 96.5 km (60 miles) away.

However, Lanzarote offers much more than that, thanks to a volcano called Timanfaya and a man called César Manrique. Both the man and the volcano have made this into a special land of huge contrasts. A quarter of Lanzarote's land area is a volcanic wasteland with its own harsh, fascinating beauty.

Around the sheltered southern shores, tourism has flourished. Yet, due to the restraining influence of the artist Manrique, development has been carefully controlled. In 1993 the whole island of Lanzarote, including all its towns and villages, was declared a UN Biosphere Reserve in recognition of its unique character and the harmony of man and nature on the island.

THE RESORTS

There are three holiday resorts on Lanzarote, the island's capital Arrecite making a fourth for a more authentic Spanish experience. The most established of the purpose-built resorts is Puerto del Carmen, a lively place, with many restaurants, late-night bars and discos. The resort extends into quieter, newer developments such as Playa de los Pocillos. On the other side of Arrecife is the second resort, Costa Teguise, which is arranged as a series of small *urbanizaciones* along the coast – some have a reputation as hideaways for well-off Spanish families, including celebrities. More remote is the third resort, Playa Blanca, steadily expanding on the southern tip of the island, which has some excellent beaches. All the resorts have good watersports facilities, with a choice of bars, restaurants and nightlife.

TIMANFAYA

The volcanic mountain Timanfaya, at 510 m (1,673 ft), dominates western Lanzarote and is responsible for the bizarre landscapes of the 50-sq-km

(19-sq-mile) Parque Nacional de Timanfaya. This is the Lanzarote *malpaís*, the island's 'badlands' where human life is all but impossible.

Though snoozing at the moment, mighty Timanfaya is still very much alive. It last blew its top 250 years ago, blasting a large part of Lanzarote into an awesome landscape of blackened, twisted rock. Today the ground at the summit is still warm to the touch, with a temperature of over 600°C (1,110°F) just below the surface. A trip to the top – whether you travel there by car, by bus or on the back of a camel – makes for *the* unmissable Lanzarote experience.

CÉSAR MANRIQUE

Few individuals have had as much influence on the culture of a place as the artist and architect César Manrique had on his native Lanzarote. Born in Arrecife on 24 April 1919, Manrique left Lanzarote to take up an art scholarship in Madrid, going on to live in New York, before returning in 1968 to his beloved Lanzarote.

César Manrique was preoccupied with the potential of tourism for good or harm, and successfully argued for strict measures to protect Lanzarote's fragile environment and culture. His greatest legacy was a law that all new buildings on the island must be low rise and traditional in design. The walls must be white, the exterior woodwork green or plain varnished wood, or blue by the sea. The visual effect is astonishing.

⬤ *César Manrique's stylish former home*

THE BEST OF LANZAROTE

The sunniest of all the Canary Islands, Lanzarote offers beautiful sandy beaches, spectacular volcanic landscapes, world-class surfing and a host of other attractions.

TOP 10 ATTRACTIONS

- Take a trip to the stunning volcanic landscapes of the **Timanfaya National Park** (page 79).

- Sunbathe and swim on the sun-baked beaches of **Puerto del Carmen** (page 59).

- Explore the exotic subterranean lake and garden of **Jameos del Agua** (page 85).

- Take in the welcome breeze on the beaches of **Costa Teguise** (page 23).

- Enjoy a walk through **Cueva de los Verdes** – part of one of the longest lava cave systems in the world (page 87).

- Soak up the atmosphere in **Puerto Calero** – one of the Mediterranean's most luxurious marinas (page 52).

- Take a boat trip to the tranquil little island of **La Graciosa** (page 89).

- Head to **Famara** beach and try your hand at windsurfing or kiteboarding (page 31).

- Explore the exotic Sunday market and imposing buildings of Lanzarote's former capital, **Teguise** (page 88).

- Visit the incredible house of **César Manrique** – built in the middle of a petrified stream of lava (page 83).

◆ *Brightly coloured boats at Puerto del Carmen*

SYMBOLS KEY

The following symbols are used throughout this book:

---

③ address **①** telephone **⑥** fax **⑩** website address **⑥** email
◐ opening times **①** important

The following symbols are used on the maps:

𝒊 information office		◯	city
✕ post office		◯	large town
▣ shopping		○	small town
✈ airport		▢	POI (point of interest)
✚ hospital		=	motorway
♦ police station		—	main road
▤ bus station		—	minor road

❶ numbers denote featured cafés, restaurants & evening venues,
& recommended tour stops

RESTAURANT CATEGORIES

The symbol after the name of each restaurant listed in this guide
indicates the price of a typical main course plus starter or dessert
and drink for one person.

£ up to €15   ££ €15–45   £££ over €45

◗ *El Golfo's green lagoon*

RESORTS
Places under the sun

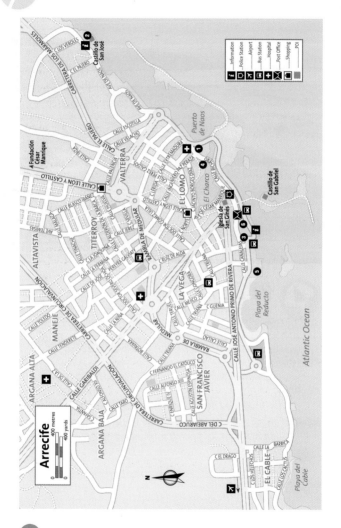

Arrecife

Arrecife

For a real taste of Spain, visit Arrecife (pronounced 'array-see-fay'), Lanzarote's waterfront capital. Home to half of the island's population, it makes few concessions to tourism and remains a bustling working town. It is the location of most of the island's commercial enterprises. The very genuine atmosphere and authentic feel of the town make a fascinating and enjoyable contrast with all Lanzarote's other resorts, and it is the only one where locals greatly outnumber visitors.

Arrecife was the birthplace and childhood home of the distinguished modern artist César Manrique. However, having been developed long before Manrique made his rulings about island architecture, it is the only town on Lanzarote with the conventional multi-storey modern buildings he deplored, including the landmark eight-storey hotel – Lanzarote's tallest building – standing on the waterfront.

Yet Arrecife also has many delightful, pretty corners and several important sights, including a surprising seawater lagoon at its heart. The town centre reaches right down to the seafront, where there is an excellent sandy beach, pleasant shaded waterfront gardens and an attractive promenade.

The capital has good hotels and makes an ideal base for exploring the island. The main street, León y Castillo, and its busy side turnings, offers some of the best shopping in Lanzarote. If you need to take a break, there are plenty of authentic tapas bars and restaurants.

Arrecife, which is the Spanish word for 'reef', dates from the early days of colonial settlement. It is guarded by two fine little waterfront fortresses, which still stand; one of them has now been transformed into a modern art museum. The town of Arrecife became Lanzarote's capital in 1852, having been gradually growing for some decades. Before that, it had long been no more than just a small fortified port serving the island's former capital, inland Teguise. To this day, many islanders refer to Arrecife as 'el puerto'.

BEACHES

Playa del Cable
For the town's second sandy beach, follow the waterfront road past del Reducto for 2 km (1 mile) to the residential district of El Cable, which fronts onto the sea and has its own 300 m (330 yd)-long beach.

Playa del Reducto
The town's excellent del Reducto main beach forms a sandy sweep along the shoreline close to the town centre. It has been awarded an EU Blue Flag for cleanliness and water quality. There are some facilities on the beach, including toilets, showers, phones and wheelchair access. Just across the road there are hotels and several bars and restaurants.

THINGS TO SEE & DO

Castillo de San Gabriel (San Gabriel Castle)
Built in 1590 to protect Arrecife's harbour, the sturdy fortress of honey-coloured stone stands a few metres offshore on the reef that gave the

⬥ *Low tide at Arrecife's harbour*

town its name. Accessed via an attractive causeway, today it lends great charm to the busy waterfront. A small archaeological museum inside displays local historic items, including Guanche art.

ⓐ Avenida Generalísimo Franco ☏ 928 81 19 50 🕔 10.00–13.00 & 16.00–19.00 Tues–Fri, 10.00–13.00 Sat; closed Sun & Mon

Castillo de San José (San José Castle)

Some 3 km (2 miles) out of town, this attractive little waterfront fortress is entered on a drawbridge. The date of its completion, 1779, is carved over the doorway. Two centuries later, César Manrique installed the International Museum of Contemporary Art. There is a roof terrace with great views, while downstairs there is an imaginative glass-walled restaurant and bar.

ⓐ Carretera de Puerto Naos ☏ 928 81 23 21 🕔 Museum 11.00–21.00; castle 11.00–24.00; restaurant 13.00–23.00

El Charco

The Charco is an inlet from the sea forming a small, still lagoon of sea water in the town centre. Today encircled by a walkway and cottages, it was the original reason for building the town here. According to legend, St Ginés lived as a hermit beside the water, and a fishing community grew up around his hermitage.

Iglesia de San Ginés (San Ginés Church)

This dignified little 18th-century church of dark volcanic stone and bright white paint, attractively restored, honours the town's patron saint. Standing in a delightful square beside the El Charco lagoon, it is still the centre of the old town, and the focal point for the locals' fiestas and celebrations.

ⓐ Plaza de San Ginés 🕔 Open for religious services only

Waterfront

East of the beach and west of the port, Arrecife's town centre reaches down to the sea in a pleasant waterfront area with shaded gardens and a promenade. The pedestrian walkway extends as far as the causeway to Castillo de San Gabriel. Just a few paces inland is the oldest part of town and the main shopping district.

ⓐ Avenida Generalísimo Franco and Avenida Mancomunidad

SHOPPING

Arrecife's main town centre shopping street is Calle León y Castillo (known locally as Calle Real), which runs down towards the waterfront. Wide, busy and crowded with strollers, it is the very heart of town. Few familiar international chains can be seen, but instead the street is lined with smaller local shops. Many good shops can also be found in side turnings off the main street.

Art & antiques

Subasta is an appealing antique shop just off the main shopping street. The helpful owner is a mine of information. ⓐ Calle Otilia Díaz 9 ⓣ 828 08 10 00

Duty-free discount stores

Many shops offer electrical and photographic goods at low, duty-free prices. Beware of fakes and goods not protected by guarantee. One of the most reliable is Visanta. ⓐ Avenida Rafael González 1

Shopping centres

El Mercadillo, in Calle León y Castillo, is the town's simple and appealing four-storey shopping centre. Inside is a diverse array of supermarkets, fashion boutiques, perfumeries and jewellers, leatherware specialists, craft shops and stores selling electrical goods at discount prices. For locals, one of the island's main shopping venues is the large indoor mall of Deiland Shopping Centre in Playa Honda, west of town. As well as a wide range of shops, it contains cafés and a cinema.

EXCURSION

Just 5 km (3 miles) from the Arrecife waterfront, leaving town on the Teguise road, is the unmissable **Fundación César Manrique**, the artist's museum and former home (see page 83).

TAKING A BREAK

Casa Ginori ££ ❶ This simple but highly recommended restaurant overlooks the fort on Puerto de Naos. Try the 'marriage' dish – grilled bass with squid. ⓐ Calle Juan de Quesada 9 ⓣ 928 80 40 45 ⓛ 13.30–16.30 & 20.00–23.30; closed Sun

Castillo de San José ££ ❷ This elegant and unusual restaurant occupies the lower floor of the modern art museum now housed inside the former fortress. Designed by Manrique with his usual flair, this imaginative glass-walled restaurant and bar offers a wide variety of excellent local and international dishes, well prepared, attractively presented and served in a remarkable setting. Smart casual dress preferred. ⓐ Carretera de Puerto Naos ⓣ 928 81 23 21 ⓛ 11.00–24.00

Domus Pompei ££ ❸ Authentic Italian cooking is served in this convivial restaurant, with an excellent choice of dishes extending beyond the usual pizza and pasta. ⓐ Calle José Betancort 19 ⓣ 928 81 42 16 ⓦ www.domuspompei.com ⓛ 12.30–16.30 & 20.00–24.00

El Leito de Proa ££ ❹ This bar and restaurant beside the waters of El Charco is very popular with locals. ⓐ Ribera del Charco 2 ⓣ 928 80 20 66 ⓛ 12.00–16.30 & 19.00–23.00. Bar opens 21.00–24.00

Restaurant Altamar £££ ❺ Solid Mediterranean and international dishes are not the only attraction here on the 17th floor of the Arrecife Gran Hotel: many also come for the magnificent panoramic views over the coast and town. ⓐ Parque Islas Canarias ⓣ 928 80 00 00 ⓦ www.arrecifehoteles.com ⓛ 13.00–15.30 & 20.00–23.30

Restaurant Chef Nizar £££ ❸ A classy restaurant with Mediterranean and Lebanese flavours – highly rated on the island. ❸ Calle Luis Morote 19 ❶ 928 80 12 60 ❸ 13.00–16.00 & 19.30–23.30

AFTER DARK

Nightlife in Arrecife is unlike what you will find in the island's three other main resorts. Instead of discos and folklore shows, the capital offers authentic evening entertainment for mainly Spanish adult audiences.

Regular bars usually stay open until the early hours. Discos generally open at around 23.00 and close at about 05.00. Instead of music from chart-topping UK bands, you will hear Spanish and Latin American music with a salsa rhythm.

The main area for discos and nightlife is Calle José Antonio in the town centre. In addition, the many clubs in Puerto del Carmen are just a few minutes' drive away. Popular Arrecife venues include:

La Biosfera ❸ Terrace Reef, Avenida Fred Olsen ❶ 928 82 41 98
Disco Pub La Panaderia ❸ Calle José Antonio 69–71

⬤ *The marble prom at Costa Teguise*

Costa Teguise

With its airy sense of space, five beaches, a wide range of sports facilities and excellent accommodation, Costa Teguise (pronounced 'teg-easy') has plenty of appeal. With an eye to Manrique's principles, the development has been cleverly zoned into green, residential and tourist areas. Purpose built on formerly empty sands just 5 km (3 miles) along the coast from Arrecife, it is now Lanzarote's second-largest resort and a favourite for upmarket, self-catering holidays, as well as having some of the island's very best hotels. Many regular visitors – including wealthy Spanish families – have bought holiday homes here. It is also ideally placed for touring and sightseeing in the north of the island.

Arranged as a ribbon of small commercial centres and *urbanizaciones* (housing developments) clinging to the seashore, Costa Teguise has different beach areas that feel quite separate from each other. The resort has aimed for a restrained and functional style; a single wide main road – Avenida del Mar in the southern half and Avenida de las Islas Canarias in the northern half – links the different districts, lined with plain and simple low-rise blocks beside the sea. It is a pity, though, that the sea cannot be seen from the road: you must use the extensive parking areas and walk between the commercial centres to reach the beaches.

Although lacking an authentic town centre or old quarter, Costa Teguise has managed to create a pleasant focus around the junction of Avenida del Jablillo and Avenida de las Islas Canarias close to little Playa del Jablillo and a few paces from the southern end of Playa de las Cucharas. This is the only place where a road reaches the sea, and there is a lively atmosphere at this point, with many shops, hotels and a variety of restaurants. Here, too, is the attractive and crowded little pedestrian square Plaza Pueblo Marinero, where visitors congregate in the balmy evening air.

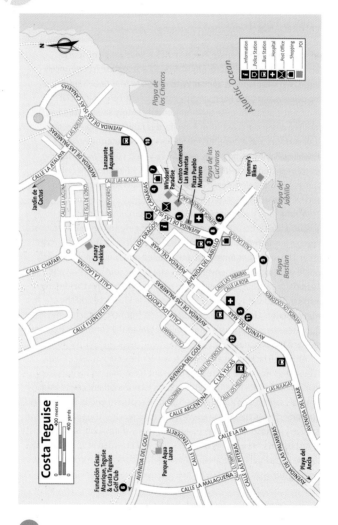

Costa Teguise

0 — 400 metres
0 — 400 yards

- Information
- Police Station
- Bus Station
- Hospital
- Post Office
- Shopping
- POI

Atlantic Ocean

Playa de los Charcos

Playa de las Cucharas

Playa del Jabillo

Playa Bastian

Playa del Ancla

Lanzarote Aquarium

Windsurf Paradise

Centro Comercial Las Maretas

Plaza Pueblo Marinero

Jardín de Cactus

Canary Trekking

Tommy's Bikes

Fundación César Manrique, Teguise & Costa Teguise Golf Club

Parque Aqua Lanza

AVENIDA DE LAS ISLAS CANARIAS
AVENIDA DE LAS PALMERAS
CALLE LA ATALAYA
CALLE LA LAGUNA
CALLE ISLA DE LOBOS
LOS HERVIDEROS
CALLE LAS ACACIAS
AVENIDA DE LAS ISLAS CANARIAS
LOS DRAGOS
AVENIDA DEL MAR
AVENIDA DE JABILLO
AVENIDA DE LAS PALMERAS
CALLE LAS TABAIBAS
CALLE LA ROSA
CALLE LAS CANARIAS
CALLE LOS COCOTEROS
CALLE CHAFARI
CALLE LA LAGUNA
CALLE FUENTECITA
CALLE LOS CROTOS
AVENIDA DE LAS PALMERAS
CALLE PANAMA
AVENIDA DEL GOLF
CALLE LOS VERDES
CALLE ARGENTINA
C COLOMBIA
C LAS YUCAS
C LAS HELECHO
AVENIDA DEL MAR
CALLE LA ISA
CALLE EL TENDERETE
CALLE LAS PITERAS
CALLE LA MALAGUEÑA
CALLE EL TIMPE
AVENIDA DE LAS PALMERAS
AVENIDA DEL MAR
C LAS AULAGAS

BEACHES

Playa del Jablillo, Playa Bastian & Playa del Ancla

All these beaches are south of the centre of Costa Teguise. They are small, breezy bays of sand and shingle backed by hotels and good-quality residential housing.

Playa de las Cucharas

The main beach is a long, sandy stretch with gardens, restaurants and hotels behind. This is the main area for windsurfing and watersports.

Playa de los Charcos

At the northern end of the resort, Los Charcos is a smaller sandy bay protected by breakwaters.

THINGS TO SEE & DO

Cycling

The rolling landscape of Lanzarote makes cycling an ideal way to see the island.

Bike Station Touring, trekking and children's BMX bikes for hire.
ⓐ Centro Comercial Las Maretas 20B ① 628 10 21 77
Ⓦ www.mylanzarote.com ⓛ 09.30–12.30 & 17.30–18.30 Mon–Fri, 10.00–12.00 & 18.00–19.00 Sat & Sun

Lanzarote Bikes You can rent bikes for any period from a day to a week or two weeks here. This centrally located shop can also provide maps, baby seats and other useful items. They also organise group excursions and guided biking tours of the island.
ⓐ Centro Comercial Las Maretas 13, Avenida de las Islas Canarias
① 651 09 60 57 Ⓦ www.lanzarote-bikes.com ⓛ 10.00–14.00; closed Sun

Tommy's Bikes The best-known cycle firm in town. This is where you can hire top-quality touring, racing and mountain bikes. They are generous with their time and advice and provide helpful maps and other information. They also organise full-day island tours and excursions, complete with sections that make use of jeeps and boats where this is necessary.

ⓐ Calle de la Goleta 16, near Galeon Playa Hotel, Playa del Jablillo
ⓣ 928 59 20 13 ⓦ www.tommys-bikes.com

Diving

There are three dive and scuba schools running out of Costa Teguise, providing equipment, courses and excursions for both beginners and more experienced divers.

Aquatis Diving Center ⓐ Playa de las Cucharas ⓣ 928 59 04 07
ⓦ www.aquatis-lanzarote.eu ⓛ 09.00–18.00

Big Blue Sea ⓣ 928 51 91 41 ⓦ www.big-blue-sea.com ⓛ 14.00–18.00; closed Sun. And the long-established **Calipso Diving** ⓐ Centro Comercial Calipso, Local 3, Avenida de las Islas Canarias ⓣ 928 59 08 79
ⓦ www.calipso-diving.com ⓔ calipso@arrakis.es
ⓛ 09.00–18.00; closed Sun

🔺 *Surf school at Costa Teguise*

Golf

The unusual and attractive 18-hole **Costa Teguise Golf Club** on the northern edge of town, designed by John Harris in 1978 and considered one of the great places in the world to play golf, is open to visitors of every ability. Lessons and equipment hire are available. This is one of two golf courses on Lanzarote, its green turf making a striking sight among cacti, palms and big geraniums and against the backdrop of the brilliant sea and sky. The charming and comfortable clubhouse has a civilised air.
ⓐ Avenida del Golf ① 928 59 05 12 Ⓦ www.lanzarote-golf.com
ⓔ lanzarotegolf@lanzarote.com

Lanzarote Aquarium

This is the biggest aquarium in the Canary Islands, with more than 30 tanks teeming with native and tropical sea creatures. The biggest draws are the shark tank and underwater tunnel – but there are also 'touching pools' where adults and children can handle sea cucumbers, starfish, sea urchins and small crabs.
ⓐ Calle Las Acacias ① 928 59 00 69
Ⓦ www.aquariumlanzarote.com ⓛ 10.00–19.00

Parque Aqua Lanza (Aqua Park)

Just follow the signs that lead away from the seafront to this enjoyable water park at the back of the town. With colourful water slides and flumes, gentle rides for the youngest toddlers, more thrilling options for teenagers and adults, a bouncy castle, a lovely pool and sunbathing area, it makes a great excursion for all the family. The water is not heated – and can be too cold for comfort in winter. There are cafés and a gift shop on the site.
ⓐ Avenida Club de Golf ① 928 59 21 28 ⓛ 10.00–18.00

Trekking

Lanzarote's network of footpaths gives unique insight into this curious environment. **Canary Trekking**, based at Costa Teguise, puts together guided walks not just for the immediate area but for all the different types of terrain around the island.

ⓐ Calle La Laguna 18, Casa 1 ☏ 609 53 76 84 (mobile)
ⓦ www.canarytrekking.com ⓔ info@canarytrekking.com

Olita Treks, also based in Costa Teguise, provide self-guided itineraries as well.

ⓐ Centro Comercial Las Maretas, Local 1 ☏ 928 59 21 48
ⓦ www.olita-treks.com ⓔ info@olita-treks.com

Windsurfing

Windsurf courses at all levels are available in several languages and offer the International Basic Windsurf Certificate, along with board rentals.

Windsurf Paradise is based on the beach at Las Cucharas. If you book in advance, you can specify the type of board you require. Trips to Famara are organised with an experienced instructor.

ⓐ Calle La Corvina 8 ☏ 928 34 60 22 & 928 59 08 62
ⓦ www.windsurflanzarote.com ⓔ info@windsurflanzarote.com
🕐 10.00–17.00 winter; 10.00–18.00 summer

EXCURSIONS

All the sights of northern Lanzarote can be easily reached from Costa Teguise, and excursions are offered by most tour operators. The Tahíche road leads to the **Fundación César Manrique** (see page 83) in just 5 km (3 miles). From here it is another 6 km (4 miles) to visit the island's former capital, **Teguise** (see page 88).

SHOPPING
Crafts market

Plaza Pueblo Marinero is the focal point of an enjoyable crafts market every Friday evening. Many of the stallholders can also be seen at the Sunday morning market at Teguise, selling items such as jewellery, pottery, stone-carvings and colourful handcrafted souvenirs.

The Guatiza road out of Costa Teguise is the route to the **Jardín de Cactus**, which is on the right after 10 km (6 miles). In the same direction, about 5 km (3 miles) further, are **Arrieta** (see page 87), **Cueva de los Verdes** (see page 87) and **Jameos del Agua** (see page 85).

TAKING A BREAK

Restaurants in Costa Teguise cluster into three distinct areas – Playa de las Cucharas, in the north of the resort; Playa del Jablillo and Plaza Pueblo Marinero, in the town centre, with many inexpensive eateries; and Playa Bastian at the southern end of the resort. It is easy to find an inexpensive meal or snack at any time at the café-bars behind the beaches.

El Patio Canario £ ❶ In the crowded pedestrian plaza near Las Cucharas beach, this inexpensive restaurant with its tables under a green awning is exceptionally good value for money, with authentic Spanish and Canarian cooking at modest prices. ⓐ El Patio Canario ☎ 928 59 11 02 🕐 12.00–24.00

Casa Blanca ££ ❷ This unusual grill restaurant in the Avenida del Jablillo area is in a charming little building with the kitchen open to view. It is surrounded by an enclosed terrace with wooden tables where local fish, salads and classic meat dishes are served. ⓐ Calle Las Olas 4 ☎ 928 59 01 55 🕐 12.00–23.30; closed Sun

Neptuno ££ ❸ Expect traditional Canarian cooking and a good range of local wines at this bright and airy restaurant. ⓐ Centro Comercial Neptuno 6, Avenida del Jablillo ☎ 928 59 03 78 🕐 13.00–16.00 & 19.00–23.00 Mon–Sat (also Sun in Aug)

Portobello ££ ❹ Excellent food and service are available at this popular restaurant at Las Cucharas beach. ⓐ Centro Comercial las Cucharas, Avenida de las Islas Canarias ☎ 928 59 02 41 🕐 13.00–23.30; closed Mon

Restaurante Isla Bonita ££ ❺ This long-established restaurant has a wide range of Canarian and Mediterranean specialities and an extensive wine list. It's popular with tourists and locals alike. ⓐ Avenida del Mar ⓣ 928 59 15 36 ⓛ 11.00–24.00; closed Sun

Restaurante Lagomar ££ ❻ Nestled in the cliffs of Nasaret, 10 km (6 miles) from Costa Teguise, this sumptuous house was designed by César Manrique and belonged to Omar Sharif (he lost it in a card game, apparently!) before being turned into a restaurant and nightclub complex. The restaurant serves classy food in a truly magical setting with rambling gardens, a lake and rooms carved from volcanic caves. Art exhibitions and live jazz on Sunday afternoons. ⓐ Calle Los Loros 6 ⓣ 928 84 56 65 ⓦ www.lag-o-mar.com ⓛ 12.00–24.00; closed Mon

La Terraza ££ ❼ The menu at this bar-restaurant with outdoor tables close to Playa de las Cucharas is geared to holiday tastes. There is an extensive children's menu with a choice of meals at low prices. ⓐ Centro Comercial las Cucharas, Avenida de las Islas Canarias 20 ⓣ 928 59 14 00 ⓛ 10.00–22.00; closed Sun

Vesubio ££ ❽ Popular Italian restaurant with great views across Punta Jablillo beach. The calzone pizza is highly recommended and the service is friendly and efficient. ⓐ Avenida del Jablillo ⓣ 928 59 00 90 ⓛ 12.00–23.30

Villa Toledo ££ ❾ Situated overlooking Playa Bastian, in the first house built in Costa Teguise, this spacious eatery offers a pool and terrace, stunning views, and accomplished fish and meat dishes cooked in a wood-burning stove. ⓐ Avenida Los Cocederos ⓣ 928 59 06 26 ⓔ villatoledo@lanzarote.com ⓛ 10.00–23.00

La Graciosa £££ ❿ This luxury restaurant is inside the smartest hotel on the island – the 5-star Gran Meliá Salinas Garden Village. A wooden walkway leads through tropical gardens into an elegant setting with live music, where the finest French cuisine is served. There are also dishes inspired by traditional local cooking, such as fish *a la sal con dos mojos*. Exceptional desserts. ⓐ Gran Meliá Salinas Garden Village, Avenida de las Islas Canarias ⓣ 928 59 00 40 ⓦ www.solmelia.com ⓔ comercial.gran.melia.salinas@solmelia.es

La Jordana £££ ⑪ In the Playa Bastian part of the resort, this is one of Costa Teguise's best restaurants, with folksy country-style décor and a fish-orientated menu that gives a local flavour to high-quality international cooking. ⓐ Calle Los Geranios 1–11 ⓣ 928 59 03 28 ⓛ 12.00–16.00 & 18.30–23.00; closed Sun

Montmartre £££ ⑫ A slightly tongue-in-cheek copy of a Parisian restaurant on the edge of town, but the skilful cooking of fine dishes such as duck liver pâté, and chicken stuffed with prawns with white wine sauce, provides the genuine feel of France. ⓐ Avenida de las Palmeras, near corner of Calle Los Geranios ⓣ 928 59 12 05 ⓛ 19.00–23.00; closed Thur

AFTER DARK

There are many bars and pubs, some with entertainment, around Playa de las Cucharas, Plaza Pueblo Marinero and Toca shopping centre (Centro Comercial Toca) on Avenida de las Islas Canarias. Many visitors to Costa Teguise feel that it is worth taking a taxi into Arrecife (5 km/3 miles), or even to Puerto del Carmen (16 km/10 miles), for evening entertainment.

Bar-restaurants **Cactus Jack's** and **Legends** are the most popular late-night entertainment venues, with stage acts such as drag shows and tribute bands. Both are in Calle Las Acacias and open daily from breakfast time until the small hours each night.

Other established evening venues are the **Robinson Beach Club** and the **Columbus Tavern**, both at the Las Cucharas commercial centre. Lively pubs around Plaza Pueblo Marinero include **Hooks** and the **Irish Fiddler**.

◔ *Kitesurfing on Famara beach*

Famara

For a taste of the simple life, unspoilt and protected Famara on the north coast makes a striking contrast with the busy resorts of the southern and eastern coasts. One of Lanzarote's best beaches is here, the 9 km (5½ mile) golden stretch of **Playa de Famara**. The spectacular **Risco de Famara** (Famara Cliffs), rising almost sheer behind the sands, create a dramatic backdrop soaring to 450 m (1,476 ft). The clifftop affords glorious views out to sea and to the offshore islands.

Visitors to Famara appreciate the wild, natural feel of the place, while many locals continue to work as farmers and fishermen. What has prevented further development here is the fact that Lanzarote's north coast has rather changeable weather and the steady breeze of the trade wind from the northwest. The ocean is more risky here, too, with some of the biggest waves anywhere around the island and strong eddies and undercurrents. However, experienced windsurfers, divers and sport fishermen love the place. Hang-gliding is another popular activity, as enthusiasts launch themselves from the top of the Famara cliffs.

Famara is also known as Lanzarote's naturist resort. About half the length of Playa de Famara is open to naturists, who can experience freedom and privacy in this natural setting. Sunbathers find shelter from sun and wind in small horseshoe-shaped enclosures of stone on the beach (similar to the *zocos* used on the island to protect grape vines).

Caleta de Famara is a small harbour village and an easy-going and uncommercialised resort at one end of Playa de Famara. It offers a wide choice of locally owned self-catering accommodation and an authentic village atmosphere. Close by, the attractive Famara *urbanización* is a self-catering holiday village of semicircular bungalows.

THINGS TO SEE & DO

Surfing

Famara is reckoned to be one of Europe's best locations for surfing due to its wave consistency, sandy beach, reliable warm air and water temperatures all year round, as well as its attractive physical setting. With these advantages, Famara is considered suitable for surfing all year round. The small beach of Playa de San Juan, west of Caleta de Famara, is also a favourite with surfers.

Calimasurf If you want to surf, surf, surf throughout your stay on the island, Calima's surf schools and surf camps at Caleta de Famara provide residential holiday courses, including 'surfaris' for different levels of ability. Stay for one to three weeks, with people at the same level as yourself. The instructors are also qualified lifeguards.
ⓐ Calle Achique 14 ⓣ 626 91 33 69 ⓦ www.calimasurf.com
ⓔ info@calimasurf.com ⓛ 10.00–21.00

Famara Surf This outfit offers surfing for all levels, with tuition, equipment hire and information on the best places to enjoy north-coast surfing to the full, ranging from world-class reef breaks to deserted beach breaks.
ⓐ Avenida el Marinero 39 ⓣ 928 52 86 76 ⓦ www.famarasurf.com
ⓔ famarasurf@hotmail.com

Surf School Lanzarote This top surfing school has more than 25 years of experience on the island, and carries the British Surfing Association's highest award (it is the only BSA Level 4 approved surf school outside the UK). Its highly qualified instructors (all of whom are also qualified lifeguards) use the latest in equipment and teaching methods for beginners and intermediates.
ⓐ Caleta de Famara ⓣ 928 52 86 23 & mobile 686 00 49 09
(09.00–10.00 & 17.00–18.00) ⓦ www.surfschoollanzarote.com
ⓔ info@surfschoollanzarote.com

EXCURSIONS

Although Famara has an away-from-it-all feeling, it is only 20 km (12 miles) from Arrecife. All the sights of northern Lanzarote can be easily visited by car from Famara, although it is necessary to go via Teguise

🔺 *Club La Santa, with its enclosed windsurfing lagoon*

(see page 88) because of the lack of other good roads. Especially within reach are **Haría** with its 'Valley of 1,000 Palms' (see page 77), continuing to **Mirador del Río** (see page 78), which is set into the same cliff face as the Risco de Famara, and, from **Orzola** (see page 87), an excursion to **La Graciosa Island** (see page 89). The **Jardín de Cactus** (see page 78) is also within easy reach, via Teseguite.

It is worthwhile travelling along the little-visited north coast to **La Santa** and beyond, and seeing the unvisited, unspoilt coastal scenery and small fishing and farming communities that survive in this part of the island.

Club La Santa, at La Santa on the north coast 12 km (7¹/₂ miles) west of Caleta de Famara, is a world-class residential sports resort, with superb equipment and facilities including an Olympic pool. It is the setting for international sports and athletics events. Day visitors are welcome at the resort, but residential stays must be booked well in advance, through your local agent. UK agent: **Sports Tours Int**.

ⓐ 91 Walkden Road, Walkden, Worsley, Manchester M28 5DQ, UK
ⓣ 0161 790 9890 ⓦ www.clublasanta.co.uk ⓔ info@clublasanta.co.uk

TAKING A BREAK

The handful of down-to-earth restaurants near the seafront at
Caleta de Famara are basic but satisfying. They generally offer fresh,
locally caught fish and seafood, with typical Canarian dishes such as
salted boiled new potatoes with *mojo* sauce (see page 98).

Las Bajas £ This very inexpensive bar-restaurant is a popular spot for
a wide range of well-prepared Spanish and international classics. Service
and cooking are of a good standard, and credit cards are accepted.
⊙ Avenida el Marinero 25 **⊙** 928 52 86 17 **⊙** 20.00–24.00; closed Mon

Casa Garcia ££ Just a little more expensive than some others, this is a
pleasant restaurant serving quality fish and seafood specialities, as well
as plenty of other dishes, including a variety of paellas. Certainly worth
a visit. **⊙** Avenida el Marinero 1 **⊙** 928 52 87 10 **⊙** 11.30–22.30; closed Mon

Restaurante El Risco £££ Serving fresh fish and paellas as well as grilled
meats, this pristine little gem provides stunning views over the ocean
towards Isla de la Graciosa. **⊙** Calle Montaña Clara 30 **⊙** 928 52 85 50
⊙ www.restauranteelrisco.com **⊙** 19.00–24.00 daily

AFTER DARK

A La Bartola This live music bar opens in the early evening and closes
when everyone leaves. **⊙** Calle Brisa 6 **⊙** 928 52 86 30

Matagorda

Despite being on the edge of Arrecife Airport – some hotel windows look onto the runway – Matagorda is surprisingly quiet and tranquil, especially in the evenings. The advantage of its location is that the transfer time for arrivals and departures is usually under 15 minutes. This is also the place to find some of the best package holiday bargains, with good modern hotel and self-catering accommodation at modest prices.

The fast national highway skirting Matagorda makes it easy to travel within a few minutes from here into the heart of Puerto del Carmen or Arrecife by car, by taxi or on the frequent buses. This gives Matagorda another much-appreciated benefit, that the island's best nightlife, bars and entertainment are readily available, yet Matagorda itself remains peaceful at night.

However, there is no necessity to leave the resort – a single commercial centre provides Matagorda with its own good selection of restaurants, bars and shops. The hotels and self-catering complexes are equipped with swimming pools and sunbathing areas, and put on their own entertainment programmes for both adults and children.

Playa de Matagorda, the resort's narrow beach, forms a pale, sandy sweep around a bright, breezy bay much loved by windsurfing and sailing enthusiasts. At high tide, the sands may in some places be completely covered, leaving the beach compact and damp after the tide withdraws, but the wide promenade provides a pleasant alternative for strolling or sunbathing.

This sunny, airy traffic-free walkway leads all the way into the next bay, **Playa de los Pocillos**, where it joins another promenade following the beach road into neighbouring **Puerto del Carmen**, 4 km (2½ miles) from Matagorda. The whole distance makes for a manageable and enjoyable walk, with plenty of bars and restaurants along the way if you want to pause for refreshment.

THINGS TO SEE & DO

Cycling

The fastest and easiest way to travel from Matagorda into Puerto del Carmen, as well as the most enjoyable, is to cycle the 4 km (2½ miles) on the wide beachside promenade. It is easy to arrange bike hire. Just ask at your hotel or apartment.

🕐 10.30–14.00

Go-karting

The excellent **Gran Karting Club Lanzarote** is a go-karting track for all ages. The senior track allows speeds up to 80 km/h (50 mph), while the junior track (for ages 12–16) gives a chance to try driving at safer speeds. There are mini-karts for the over-fives, while children over ten can also try their hand on mini-motorcycles called mini-bikes.

🅐 Carretera de las Playas LZ-2, Km 7 🅣 619 75 99 46
🅦 www.grankarting.com 🕐 10.00–21.00

Watersports

Matagorda is among the best bays on the south coast for windsurfing and sailing. There is equipment hire on the beach for windsurfing and snorkelling, and boat trips for big-game fishing expeditions.

> ### SHOPPING
> The extensive shopping areas at the heart of Arrecife (see page 18) and Puerto del Carmen (see page 59) are just minutes away by taxi or bus.
> **Centro Comercial Matagorda** The resort's own pedestrian shopping complex offers a range of souvenirs and beach paraphernalia.
> **Deiland** This shopping centre on the main road into Arrecife is much used by locals. Here you will find a good selection of shops selling all kinds of goods, as well as cafés and bars.

● *Playa de Matagorda*

EXCURSIONS

Be sure to take the short trip into Arrecife (see page 15) to look round all the sights in the island's capital. Organised excursions to Timanfaya and the other sights around the island generally leave from Puerto del Carmen, a few minutes' drive away by bus or taxi, or your tour operator may provide a bus pick-up.

TAKING A BREAK

There are several bars and eating places in the Matagorda commercial centre, including Chinese, Italian, Indian and British ones. For a much bigger choice of restaurants, take a bus or taxi into nearby Arrecife (see page 19) or Puerto del Carmen (see page 62).

Steve's Balti House £ With a very British atmosphere, apart from the outdoor tables, Steve's restaurant in Matagorda commercial centre serves an extensive menu of tasty, typical balti cuisine, including plenty of seafood, meat and vegetarian dishes. There is also a full takeaway service with free delivery within the resort.
ⓐ Centro Comercial Matagorda ❶ 928 51 09 87 ⓛ 18.30–24.00
❶ Free delivery

AFTER DARK

Matagorda's nightlife is fairly low key. Hotels and accommodation complexes put on entertainment or stage shows several evenings a week. There is a small selection of pubs and bars in the Matagorda commercial centre.

Bar Rockola £ Among the bars in the Matagorda commercial centre, Bar Rockola plays popular music of the 50s, 60s and 70s, country-and-western, and rock and roll. A giant screen shows the latest top sporting events. Wines, cocktails, teas and coffees are served all day.
ⓐ Centro Comercial Matagorda ❶ 636 13 54 37 ⓛ 19.00–02.00 Mon–Fri, 12.00–04.00 Sat & Sun

The New Inn £ Describing itself as a traditional family pub, this convivial establishment in Matagorda commercial centre offers an extremely full range of entertainment for a pleasant evening out, including disco and karaoke, six TV screens for sports enthusiasts, quizzes and other games, and a wide range of drinks. ⓐ Centro Comercial Matagorda
ⓛ 17.00 till late Mon–Fri, 13.00 till late Sat & Sun

Playa Blanca

The southern coastline of Lanzarote forms a huge, gently curving, sheltered bay, reaching 9 km (5½ miles) across from **Pechiguera Point** in the west to **Papagayo Point** in the east. This in turn is divided into three smaller bays, each of which has a sandy beach and rocky outcrops. At the centre of this coast, and rapidly spreading in both directions, lies Lanzarote's third-largest resort.

Playa Blanca occupies a sunny, sheltered position with exquisite, ever-changing views across shimmering blue water towards neighbouring Fuerteventura and, in front of it, tiny Lobos Island.

The focal point of Playa Blanca remains the picturesque former fishing village at its western end, with its alleys and paved lanes. Arguably, though, the resort's greatest attraction is the pedestrianised promenade beside sandy beaches.

Set back from the waterfront are some of the most comfortable and architecturally pleasing modern hotels on the island, which show the potential of imaginative designers who work within the guidelines laid down by César Manrique. Many are almost self-contained, with their own shops, restaurants, pools, sunbathing areas and direct beach access.

In addition, Lanzarote's most southerly resort has a quietly civilised atmosphere, with a privileged and relaxed air, good watersports facilities and better-than-average restaurants. Because the island's other three big towns are so close to each other, Playa Blanca also has something of a remote feel about it, even though it is just a 30-minute drive from Puerto del Carmen.

The port itself, with ferries to other islands, remains a vibrant feature of the town. At the other end of town, the latest waterside amenity is an attractive pleasure harbour, **Marina Rubicón** with 400 berths, where luxury yachts are moored.

There are good beaches in the centre of Playa Blanca, but dedicated seekers of sun and sand head out of town on the rough roads to several bigger and better stretches nearby, especially **Papagayo** to the east.

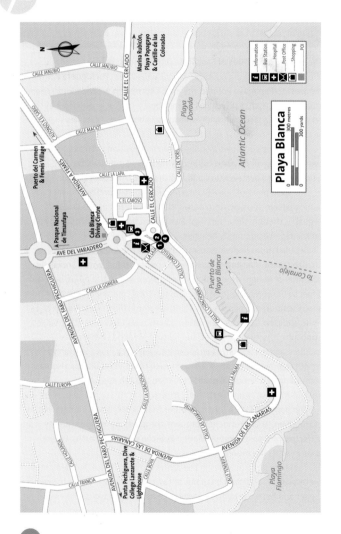

BEACHES

Playa Blanca

The name of the town means 'white beach', but the sands of the sheltered town centre bay are golden in colour. The beach is safe for swimming, backed by an attractive promenade, and has been awarded an EU Blue Flag for cleanliness.

Playa Dorada

In the first bay east of the town centre, this is Playa Blanca's second beach. An EU Blue Flag winner, it is an attractive curve of gently shelving golden sand in a sheltered sun-trap position. Behind is a beach bar where you can hire umbrellas and sunloungers.

Playa Flamingo

This is one of the fine sandy bays, safe for swimming, beyond the harbour west of the town. A promenade links the beach to the harbour.

Playa Papagayo

Reached along a bumpy track (or, preferably, by boat from the harbour), the wide, beautiful unspoilt sands of Playa Papagayo lie about 5 km (3 miles) east of town beyond Castillo de las Coloradas. Considered among Spain's best beaches, it remains undeveloped, despite being a popular haunt for sun-seeking day trippers. There are several other more secluded sandy bays to either side of Papagayo Point, including the favourite for nude sunbathing, **Playa de Puerto Muelas**. There is a simple beach bar at Playa Papagayo, but no other facilities, so take plenty of drinks and food.

THINGS TO SEE & DO

Boat trips

Leisure cruises from Playa Blanca leave several times a day, including outings to Papagayo beach as well as catamaran excursions,

a child-orientated pirate cruise and the schooner *Marea Errota*
(☎ 928 517 63 ✉ mareaerrota@retemail.es) and deep-sea fishing
excursions. ⏰ 09.00–19.00

Castillo de las Coloradas
Projecting from the Punta del Águila headland just east of Playa Blanca,
this fine circular watchtower was first built in 1769 as a lookout to help
protect Lanzarote from raiders and pirates. Reconstructed in 1778, its
main role today is to give wonderful views across to Fuerteventura.
⏰ Always open ❗ Free access

Diving
The **Marina Rubicón Diving Center** offers daily diving trips to more
than 30 exclusive dive sites, including the island of Fuerteventura and
the little Isla de Lobos off the north of Fuerteventura, plus 'Learn to Dive'
courses of three to five days' duration.

◆ *Colourful boats in the Old Port*

ⓐ Puerto Deportivo Marina Rubicón ❶ 928 34 93 46
ⓦ www.rubicondiving.com ⓔ info@rubicondiving.com
🕘 08.30–18.30 Mon–Sat; closed Sun
Dive College Lanzarote (ⓐ Centro Comercial La Mulata,
Urbanización Montaña Roja ❶ 928 51 86 68
ⓦ www.scubalanzarote.co.uk 🕘 09.00–18.00) is a leading dive centre
running underwater excursions to discover wrecks, caverns and reefs, as
well as astonishing marine life such as rays, scorpion fish and angel
sharks. It also offers a wide range of PADI courses from beginner to
instructor level.

In modern, well-equipped premises 50 m (55 yds) from Playa Dorada
beach is **Cala Blanca Diving Centre**, founded by Spanish professionals
and providing a diverse choice of diving trips, with qualified guides, as
well as diving courses for all levels. ⓐ Centro Comercial El Papagayo
❶ 928 51 90 40 & mobile: 607 30 12 30 ⓦ www.calablancasub.com
🕘 08.30–19.00; closed Sun

Marina Rubicón

Opened in 2003 on the Papagayo side of Playa Blanca, Marina Rubicón
has already become among the Canaries' most prestigious moorings.
The area preserves a traditional architectural style, and there are a
number of restaurants, bars and boutiques.
ⓐ Puerto Deportivo Marina Rubicón, Urbanización Castillo del Águila
❶ 928 51 90 12 ⓦ www.marinarubicon.com

Old Port (also known as el Varadero)

Not only ferries and pleasure cruisers come and go at the bustling port –
working fishermen make full use of it, too. Watch as they bring in their
catch on the quayside, then sample it in the nearby restaurants that
overlook the harbour.

The promenade

Playa Blanca's attractive beachside promenade extends along the whole
distance from the Old Port in the west of the resort to the Marina

Rubicón in the east. After dark, the lights of Corralejo, on Fuerteventura, can be seen on the horizon.

Walking

Southern Lanzarote is great country for keen walkers. From Playa Blanca there are scenic, easily followed coastal paths to the Pechiguera lighthouse in the west, and Papagayo in the east, both about 5 km (3 miles) away. Allow an hour each way and take plenty of water.

EXCURSIONS

Femés village

The village church in this quiet inland hill village near Playa Blanca was the first cathedral in the whole of the Canary Islands. Serious walkers can climb from the village to the panoramic Atalaya de Femés for views of Timanfaya in one direction and Fuerteventura in the other. Enjoy one of the best sunset spots on the island.

⬥ *A view from the rocks of Isla de Lobos*

Fuerteventura

Ferries travel between Playa Blanca and Corralejo on Fuerteventura
regularly throughout the day (see page 93 for more details). The channel
between the two islands is just 11 km (7 miles) and the trip takes about
25 minutes.

Grand Tour

Offered by most inclusive holiday operators to Playa Blanca, and also
available from local travel agencies, the Grand Tour is a day-long
excursion from the resort to several of Lanzarote's major sights.
Included are the **Timanfaya** volcano drive, a tasting at **La Geria**
winery, a trip to **Jameos del Agua** (see page 85), and a lunch stop.

Parque Nacional de Timanfaya

Playa Blanca is well placed for the sights of western Lanzarote, including
Yaiza (see page 66) and **Timanfaya** (see page 79), just a 20-minute
drive away.

TAKING A BREAK

There is a selection of relaxed cafés and bars serving food all day along
the promenade close to the harbour, on the beachside walkway and
around the marina. Standards are generally high, but check first if you
want to pay by credit card.

Brisa Marina ££ ❶ On the promenade close to the old village
and harbour, this restaurant is much liked for its excellent fresh
fish and seafood dishes, including both international classics and

Canarian specialities. ⓐ Paseo Marítimo 24 ⓣ 928 51 72 06
ⓛ 10.00–23.00

El Almacén de la Sal £££ ❷   A converted salt store provides a cool stone and timber setting for this restaurant, with the best of fresh fish and meat dishes, including international, Spanish and Canarian specialities. Shaded terrace outside, and sometimes live music. ⓐ Avenida Marítima 12 ⓣ 928 51 78 85 ⓦ www.almacendelasal.com ⓛ 11.00–23.00; closed Tues

La Bocaina £££ ❸   After trading for more than 40 years, La Bocaina has built up a loyal following of locals and returning holidaymakers. Diners are lured by the talents of the two British chefs-owners, serving dishes like poached sole and *tournedos Rossini*, and also the views across the Bocaina Straits. ⓐ El Varadero 4 ⓣ 928 52 83 88 ⓦ www.labocainarestaurant.com ⓛ 12.00–20.30

Restaurante Casa Pedro £££ ❹   This classy restaurant mixes international and Canarian flavours to a very high standard – one of the best on the island. ⓐ Avenida Marítima ⓣ 928 51 79 65 ⓛ 12.00–22.30; closed Thur

AFTER DARK

The promenade in Playa Blanca is the heart of evening activity, mainly consisting of restaurants and convivial bars. The hotels have comfortable bars, sometimes with easy-listening live music. After dinner, many of the hotels and self-catering complexes offer stage shows, typically along the lines of Russian dancers, magic shows and tribute bands. Central Playa Blanca becomes quiet at night and is not the right choice for anyone who wants to dance until breakfast time, although there is a disco at **Punta Limones**, west of the resort centre. The nearest all-night music and dance venues are 30 km (19 miles) away in **Puerto del Carmen**.

Playa de los Pocillos

The huge, sandy sweep of Pocillos bay is one of the best beaches on the island. At high tide it is largely covered with water, leaving it damp for a while when the tide pulls back – hence its name (pronounced 'pothiyoss'), which means 'puddle beach'. However, it quickly dries again in the warm breeze that blows onto this shore, making it a haven for windsurfers as well as sunbathers.

Pocillos lies just beyond the eastern end of the island's main resort, Puerto del Carmen. It has become a quiet suburb of its livelier, larger neighbour, which is easily accessible on foot (about 20 minutes) on the waterside pavement, or by taxi. In the other direction, a pleasant beachside promenade runs round to Matagorda in the next bay.

Most of the wide range of hotel and self-catering accommodation choices at Playa de los Pocillos are of a good standard and excellent value for money. Many villas set back from the sea are second homes belonging to prosperous Spanish owners from the mainland.

The area is popular with families with young children, and those seeking a peaceful alternative to the more hectic Puerto del Carmen – while still being within walking distance of all its amenities.

There is no need, however, to depend on Puerto del Carmen. At the centre of the Pocillos beachside development, the **Costa Mar** commercial centre has a selection of shops and restaurants. It also has a disco and a couple of bars. At the northern end of the beach, the more upmarket commercial centre **Los Jameos Playa** is an attractive row of shops and high-quality restaurants.

THINGS TO SEE & DO

Quad-biking

Among Lanzarote's top names for hire of quad-bikes, Pocillos-based **MegaFun Bikes** also run day trips and safaris all over the island. Ⓐ Centro Comercial Costa Mar Ⓣ 928 51 28 93 Ⓦ www.megafun-lanzarote.com Ⓔ info@megafun-lanzarote.com

Watersports

Playa de los Pocillos is a magnet for watersports enthusiasts from all over the island. You'll find many activities available on the huge sandy bay. Try your hand at jet-skiing, or hop on a banana boat and test your balance on the briny. By far the most popular sport at Playa de los Pocillos is windsurfing and there is board rental from beach outlets here or along the boardwalk at Puerto del Carmen. Or bring your own equipment!

TAKING A BREAK

Casa Carmen £ An inexpensive little place opposite the Hotel San Antonio, this restaurant serves a wide range of dishes including chicken fajita and Mexican dishes. ⓐ Centro Comercial Costa Luz, Avenida de las Playas ⓣ 928 51 23 29 ⓛ 11.00–24.00; closed Sun

Leneghans £ This sea-view restaurant offers an unusual combination of Irish and Canarian cuisine, and next door is a lively Irish pub. ⓐ Centro Comercial Los Pocillos ⓣ 928 52 84 23 ⓛ 10.00–24.00

Pizzeria Italica ££ For tasty classic Italian dishes, including charcoal-oven pizza and tasty pasta, this authentic and atmospheric restaurant has a friendly atmosphere and modest prices. ⓐ Centro Comercial Jameos Playa ⓣ 928 59 60 77 ⓛ All day

O Botafumeiro £££ In the Costa Luz centre, this first-class seafood restaurant is more French than Spanish in style. Try excellent *calamares*, or sample the steak *al roquefort*. Private parking. ⓐ Calle Alemania 9 ⓣ 928 51 15 03 ⓔ botafumeiro2308@hotmail.com ⓛ 12.00–16.30 & 19.00–24.00; closed Mon

Playa Quemada

It is a testimony to Lanzarote's lack of rampant development that there are still south-coast waterfront villages that have not yet been taken over by tourism. Playa Quemada (pronounced 'kemarda'), reached by a 4-km (2½-mile) road from the Tías highway, remains virtually undiscovered.

Due partly to its off-the-beaten-track position, Playa Quemada remains a small and simple traditional fishing village of attractive low, white houses, giving a fascinating insight into the Lanzarote of some decades ago. Lying in a calm and sheltered sunny bay protected from strong winds or currents, its seafront, situated beyond the houses, is a beach of dark volcanic rock and stones. Fishermen's boats are moored here.

Although this perhaps makes a poor comparison with the pale sands of the other resorts, it shelves gently into the calm waters and is excellent for swimming. The greatest advantage is the absence of crowds of holidaymakers, except for a few, mainly Spanish, aficionados who have discovered this secret place. A better beach can be reached by a short walk over the cliffs or, at low tide, along the shore.

● *A dramatic seascape from the beach at Playa Quemada*

There are, however, a few caravans, as well as several upmarket second homes and holiday villas here, enjoying spectacular ocean views towards neighbouring **Fuerteventura** and Isla de Lobos.

For a relaxing escape into sunshine and the simple life, with nothing but fresh-air outdoor activities to distract you from the sunlounger, Playa Quemada is a real find. For sailing enthusiasts, the village is next to the smart marina resort of **Puerto Calero** (11 km/7 miles by road). Yet if you feel the need for shopping, entertainment and nightlife, the island's main resort, **Puerto del Carmen**, is only 15 km (9$^1/_2$ miles) away.

BEACHES

Apart from the rocky Playa Quemada seashore, it is possible to follow footpaths around small headlands to reach other bays and beaches. The nearest, **Playa de la Arena**, is a beach of black sand just a few minutes' walk from **Playa Quemada**. It is popular for nude sunbathing.

THINGS TO SEE & DO

Diving
Based in nearby Puerto Calero, the Dive Centre run by **Island Watersports** is highly respected for its varied and professional dives under the supervision of highly qualified instructors. Among the dives on offer are trips to Playa Quemada to explore the Quemada Ledges, diving into shallow or deep water as preferred over a rocky reef. Taking the deeper option (down to 28 m/92 ft), there are ledges where large fish such as angel sharks and stingrays can be seen, as well as numerous small fish such as damselfish, wrasse and bream. Quemada Menor is a fascinating, more shallow dive on a smaller reef, where large shoals of sardines, sea cucumbers and barracuda can be seen. The Dive Centre is both a BSAC School and a PADI Dive Centre, offering courses from introductory dives for the absolute beginner up to more advanced courses.

ⓐ Puerto Calero Marina ⓣ 928 51 18 80 ⓦ www.divelanzarote.com
ⓔ info@divelanzarote.com ⓒ 09.30–18.00; closed Sun

Horse riding

Lanzarote a Caballo, located on the main highway between the Puerto Calero and Playa Quemada junctions, is an equestrian activity centre offering horse riding for all levels at the site, for exploring the local countryside on horseback or for guided sightseeing tours of the island. At an entertaining children's park called **Fort Apache**, activities with horses and ponies can be enjoyed. The site has its own restaurant, **La Caravana** (see below).

ⓐ Carretera Arrecife–Yaiza, Km 17 ❶ 928 83 00 38 ❶ 928 81 39 95
ⓦ www.lanzaroteacaballo.com ⓔ lanzaroteacaballo@lanzarote.com
❶ 10.00–18.00

Walking

This is an exceptional area for exploring the south coast on foot, with fairly well-marked coastal and hill paths. In Playa Quemada, follow the main street uphill and continue out of the village, where the road becomes a track. This leads over the hills on a relatively easy, but thrilling, walk to **Puerto Calero** (see page 52).

EXCURSIONS

Playa Quemada is close to the inland volcanic wine-growing region **La Geria** (see page 76), the picturesque village of **Yaiza** (see page 66) on the edge of the *malpaís*, and **Parque Nacional de Timanfaya** (see page 79).

TAKING A BREAK

Playa Quemada has a handful of tapas bars and a few small restaurants specialising in good fish and seafood at low prices. The nearest wider choice of restaurants is at Puerto Calero (11 km/7 miles away).

La Caravana ££ Enjoy a range of tasty meat dishes in a fascinating setting at the restaurant in the Lanzarote a Caballo riding and activity centre. It is on the main road between the Playa Quemada and Puerto Calero junctions. ⓐ Carretera Arrecife–Yaiza, Km 17 ❶ 928 83 00 38 ❶ 10.00–18.00

Puerto Calero

One of Europe's most prestigious yacht marinas clings to the rocky coast south of Puerto del Carmen. It displays to the full the appeal of Lanzarote to a chic, well-to-do crowd, including many wealthy Spanish families. The harbour has 420 floating wharves capable of berthing boats of from 8 to 75 m (26 to 246 ft) in length, and a ravishing selection of luxury craft can often be seen moored here. To add to the scene, dark hills rise steeply behind, and huge shoals of bright fish swim among the yachts floating in the perfectly clear waters.

Puerto Calero has quickly established itself as one of Europe's most beautiful marinas. It occupies a magnificent setting, literally blasted out

◆ *Puerto Calero's pristine marina*

of the dark rocks of this glorious stretch of coastline, and has the appeal to yachtsmen of a safe berth for Atlantic sailing in African latitudes. Although Lanzarote's best-known artist was César Manrique, another of the island's sons is the acclaimed modern architect Luis Ibáñez Margalef. It was Margalef who first conceived and designed this attractive harbour in the 1980s.

However, a dramatic change came a decade later with the decision to double the size of the marina, a project that came to fruition in 2001. Puerto Calero turned from being a sailing paradise into a fully fledged resort, with two luxury hotels and a range of comfortable detached and semi-detached self-catering villas. True to Manrique's guidelines, all the accommodation is in step with the island's traditional architecture and is sensitive to the surrounding environment.

To enjoy Puerto Calero, there is no need to be a keen yachtsman or even to step on board a boat at all. Many day visitors arrive by road, and have come simply to stroll, or to enjoy a lazy lunch on the terrace of one of the many excellent bars and restaurants on the quayside. In addition to the resort's marine activities, there are sports facilities, an art gallery and a museum.

BEACHES

Puerto Calero has no beach of its own, but **Puerto del Carmen** is just 5 km (3 miles) away on the new direct road.

THINGS TO SEE & DO

Catamaran excursions
Sample the good life for a day on a luxury 23m (75ft) skippered catamaran with a professional crew. No previous sailing experience is needed and there are family sailings or adult-only trips to choose from. The cats sail from the marina along the coast to Playa Blanca and a break at Papagayo beach. Bar service, lunch, snorkelling equipment and a jet-ski ride are all included in the trip.

@ Puerto Calero marina ☎ 928 51 30 22 ⓦ www.catlanza.com
@ info@catlanza.com 🕐 09.00–1800 winter; 08.30–20.00 summer
❶ Free bus

Diving

Puerto Calero's highly professional **Dive Centre** organises BSAC and PADI courses from introductory dives for the absolute beginner up to advanced, and dives around the island for all abilities. Depending on currents, it is also possible to travel to a small wreck.
@ Puerto Calero marina ☎ 928 51 18 80 ⓦ www.divelanzarote.com

Fishing excursions

Visitors who are keen to try big-game fishing can choose from a number of companies. **Lanzarote Fishing Club**, based at the marina, offer outings in specially designed boats under the supervision of experienced skipper Tino García.
@ Calle Camino del Mesón 49B ☎ 636 47 40 00 🖷 928 51 43 78
ⓦ www.lanzarotefishingclub.net
@ tinogarcia@lanzarotefishingclub.com 🕐 09.00–14.30

Galería de Arte Puerto Calero (Puerto Calero Art Gallery)

The inspiration for this ambitious gallery derives from the principles of César Manrique – to create a harmonious interaction between art, landscape, local culture and the visitor. The museum's aim is to acquire and promote the work of local artists.
@ Puerto Calero marina ☎ 928 51 15 05
ⓦ http://galeriadearte.puertocalero.com
@ galeriadearte@puertocalero.com 🕐 16.00–21.00

Museo de Cetáceos de Canarias (Canarian Cetacean Museum)

Cetaceans are the whale and dolphin family. The Canarian Cetacean Museum, housed inside a former dry dock, offers visitors the chance to discover one of Europe's major cetacean collections. Here they can experience the Canary Islands' ocean setting and learn about these remarkable creatures through images, sound, full-size replicas and biological exhibits. There is also a gift shop.

ⓐ Edificio Antiguo Varadero, Local 11 ❶ 928 84 95 60 ❻ 928 84 95 61
Ⓦ www.museodecetaceos.org ⓔ info@museodecetaceos.org
🕑 10.00–18.00

Submarine Safaris

Come on board the modern 18.5 m (61 ft)-long submarine *Sub Fun Tres* and descend into a magical marine world. The sub is air-conditioned, with air pressure at normal atmospheric levels. A highly professional crew provides an unforgettable outing. No children under two years.

ⓐ Submarine Safaris SL, Puerto Calero marina ❶ 928 51 28 98
& 928 51 29 06 Ⓦ www.submarinesafaris.com
ⓔ info@submarinesafaris.com 🕑 Excursions at 10.00, 12.00, 14.00 & 16.00

Watersports

A wide range of rentals for watersports at the marina includes jet-ski hire and paracraft.

🔺 *Boats in the harbour at Puerto Calero*

TAKING A BREAK

McSorley's Irish Bar £ This friendly and enjoyable pub serves food and drink all day and into the evening, including familiar beers from home as well as local brews. The menu is British, offering the best of pub food. Nightly entertainment. ⓐ Puerto Calero marina ⓣ 680 42 46 65

La Taberna del Puerto £ A quality tapas bar that draws in locals and tourists with its fresh seafood dishes. ⓐ Lugar del Puerto Calero ⓣ 928 51 28 82

El Tomate £ This pleasant and useful little café has outdoor tables with a view of the boats coming and going. A good spot for a quick snack, *bocadillos* (see page 100) or tapas. ⓐ Calle Teide ⓣ 928 51 22 10 ⓛ 11.00–23.00

La Pappardella ££ At the far end of the promenade, this is one of Lanzarote's best Italian restaurants. Service is friendly yet efficient, and prices are very moderate. ⓐ Paseo Marítimo ⓣ 928 51 29 11 ⓛ 12.00–01.00

Restaurante Amura ££ This very popular and attractive place to meet friends and relax offers a wide range of well-prepared à la carte international dishes. There are good sea views both from inside and from the large terrace. ⓐ Puerto Calero marina ⓣ 928 51 31 81 ⓕ 928 51 14 62 ⓛ 13.00–23.00; closed Mon

AFTER DARK

The marina's restaurants and bars remain open until late in Puerto Calero. For late-night discos and clubs, travel the 5 km (3 miles) into **Puerto del Carmen**.

Puerto del Carmen

Lanzarote's principal resort is the focal point for all its energetic youth-orientated nightlife, and there is a lively, busy holiday scene during the day. However, even here, the island keeps its unique charm. The strict guidelines laid down by artist César Manrique have prevented the building of any high-rise hotels, so Puerto del Carmen retains a delightfully low-key, small-town feel. Most buildings are only two storeys high and have traditional white walls and painted woodwork.

⬤ *The beach at Puerto del Carmen*

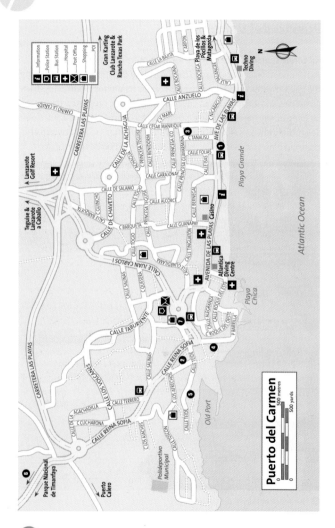

Puerto del Carmen

SHOPPING

The many small shops along the **Avenida de las Playas** sell a huge variety of craft goods, souvenirs, beachwear, sports goods, perfumes and fashions. There are similar boutiques in the **old town**, and some are worth looking at for attractive, unusual summer clothes. Several shops, known as *bazares*, claim to be selling top-brand electrical and photographic goods at cut prices. These should be treated with caution by the inexperienced, although it is sometimes possible to pick up a genuine bargain.

The resort consists of little more than a single long main street, Avenida de las Playas, running right beside the sea. On one side of the Avenida there is a string of enticing open-fronted eateries, bars and shops; the other side is mainly devoted to a delightful flower-decked promenade, alongside landscaped gardens and a vast beach of golden sand.

Where the main beach ends, the promenade continues to a rockier foreshore, a smaller beach and yet more beautiful sea views. At the southern end of the resort, an older district of quaint lanes clusters around the picturesque little port that gives the town its name. The original Old Port survives today as a bustling restaurant district with a good deal of authentic Spanish flavour. The promenade continues north beyond **Puerto del Carmen** into neighbouring **Playa de los Pocillos** and **Matagorda**. The easiest way to get from one beach to the next is on foot or by bicycle, but taxis and frequent buses also connect the three resorts.

BEACHES

Playa Grande, the very spacious, safe and sandy main beach in the centre of the resort, has an EU Blue Flag for cleanliness and water quality. There are sunloungers and umbrellas are for hire.

THINGS TO SEE & DO

Diving

The combination of Lanzarote's warm, clear waters, varied marine life and a number of wrecks sunk nearby make diving a very attractive activity when staying in Puerto del Carmen. Among established dive centres that arrange diving excursions and offer training courses are **Atlantica Diving Centre** (ⓐ jetty of Hotel Los Fariones, Calle Acatife ⓘ 928 51 07 17 Ⓦ www.atlanticadiving.es) and **Techno Diving** (ⓐ Centro Comercial Matagorda ⓘ 928 51 56 47 Ⓦ www.techno-diving.com ⓛ daily).

⬥ *The Old Port at Puerto del Carmen*

Game fishing

Lanzarote is known for its rich fishing and Puerto del Carmen is a good place for arranging to join a game fishing expedition to catch blue marlin tuna, swordfish or bonito.

Go-karting

Close to Matagorda, on the main highway just past the Puerto del Carmen turn-off, **Gran Karting Club Lanzarote** is an excellent track for visitors of all ages. The senior track allows speeds up to 80 km/h (50 mph), while the junior track (for ages 12–16) allows for driving at safer speeds. There are mini-karts for the over-fives, and children over ten can also try their hand on mini-motorcycles.

ⓐ Carretera las Playas ☏ 619 75 99 46 Ⓦ www.grankarting.com
🕐 10.00–21.00 winter; 10.00–22.00 summer

Old Port (also known as El Varadero)

Where the beach ends, the resort's waterfront becomes a tangled area of old lanes leading to a delightful little former fishing port, the original Puerto del Carmen. There are still fishing boats in the harbour, as well as leisure craft and larger boats, and many strollers by the waterside, all together creating a bustling and enjoyable scene. A string of bars and restaurants, some climbing to terraces with wide views, runs alongside the port.

Puerto Calero

Be sure to take in a trip – by road or by water or even on a clifftop footpath – to this attractive upmarket marina lying just 5 km (3 miles) away from Puerto del Carmen. It makes an enjoyable outing even if only to sit with a coffee and admire the smart yachts at their moorings. See page 53 for details of the many facilities for watersports, leisure activities and boat excursions available at the marina.

Rancho Texas Park

Rancho Texas is an activity and leisure centre based on horse riding, but with a lot of other entertainment on a Wild West theme, including lively country-and-western nights with music, dancing and barbecues. Sights include an 'Indian village', 'Medicine Man Cave', 'Goldmine' and a collection of American animals. There are shows with birds of prey and alligators several times daily. Among the horse-riding options are a three-hour trek for experienced riders and a one-hour trek designed for beginners. There are three restaurants on the site.

🅐 Calle Noruega, Tías 🕿 928 84 12 86
🌐 www.ranchotexaslanzarote.com 🄴 ranchotexas@lanzarote.com
🕔 09.30–17.30

Watersports

There is equipment hire on the beach for windsurfing, jet-skis and other watersports. Basic tuition is given.

EXCURSIONS

The resort is ideally placed for touring in both the north and south of the island. Tour operators and local agencies offer half-day and full-day excursions from the resort to all the main sights of the island, especially Lanzarote's number one sight, the beautiful **Parque Nacional de Timanfaya** (see page 79). Early on Sunday mornings, coaches leave Puerto del Carmen for the big weekly crafts market in the inland town of **Teguise** (see page 88).

TAKING A BREAK

For more character and classier cooking (but with higher prices), the **Old Port** is usually the best choice for a good lunch or dinner. Catering more to simple family dining, the **Avenida de las Playas** is said to have around 200 restaurants along its length. Most display pictures outside of what is on offer, usually familiar favourites such as pizza, steak and chips, or spaghetti bolognese. Few accept reservations – just choose one you like and take a seat.

El Mirador £ ❶   One of the only bar-restaurants on the beach side of the Avenida. A perfect spot to enjoy a drink or lunch with a wonderful sea view. ⓐ Opposite Centro Comercial Arena Dorada, Avenida de las Playas

La Bodega ££ ❷   This tapas bar-restaurant is just a stone's throw away from the Old Port. It has a comprehensive wine list. ⓐ Calle Roque Nublo 5 ❶ 928 51 29 53 ❶ 13.00–24.00

La Cañada £££ ❸   This well-established restaurant off the Avenida is considered one of Lanzarote's best places for fine dining. On the menu is a range of tasty meat, fish and seafood dishes. Air-conditioned. ⓐ Calle César Manrique 2–3 ❶ 928 51 04 15 ❶ 928 51 21 08 ⓔ lacaniadalanza@terra.es ❶ 12.00–24.00; closed Sun eve

Casa Tino El Sardinero £££ ❹   Among the most highly praised fish restaurants in Puerto del Carmen, this relaxed, unpretentious and informal place is in the port area at the west end of the seafront (but with little or no sea view). Choose grilled sardines or *sancocho*, for example, or you can just point out the fish you want – come early for a good choice. ⓐ Calle Nuestra Señora del Carmen 2 ❶ 928 51 16 09 ❶ 10.00–00.30

El Puerto Viejo £££ ❺   Top dining in the Old Port area at this grill restaurant, whose acclaimed chef, Luis León Romero, uses the best and freshest of local ingredients to make a range of international and local specialities. Good sea views, and décor is on an appropriately maritime theme. ⓐ Avenida del Varadero ❶ 928 51 52 65 ❶ 12.30–16.00 & 18.30–23.30

La Tegala £££ ❻   State-of-the-art cuisine and seriously good views are laid on here in this restored stone house about 3 km (2 miles) away from Puerto del Carmen. ⓐ Carretera Tías–Yaiza 60 ❶ 928 52 45 24 ⓦ www.lategala.com ❶ 14.00–16.30 & 20.00–23.30; closed Sun

El Tomate £££ ❼ Famed for its high standard of international cuisine and frequented by local dignitaries, this popular eatery is always busy and reservations are recommended. ⓐ Calle los Jameos ❶ 928 51 19 85 Ⓦ www.eltomate-lanzarote.com 🕐 19.00–22.30

AFTER DARK

After dark, Avenida de las Playas becomes Lanzarote's busiest entertainment district. The focal point is the **Centro Atlántico**, about halfway along the avenue. Here, there is something for most tastes and budgets, ranging from convivial pubs and cocktail bars to cabaret venues, nightclubs and all-night dance clubs.

Casino
Play the slot machines during the day at the Casino, or dress up and come at night to gamble your holiday money in its gaming rooms where roulette and blackjack are played. There is a restaurant, bar and cabaret entertainment. The Casino is not glamorous, but all guests must be over 18, be appropriately dressed and have their passport with them.
ⓐ Centro Ocio, Avenida de las Playas 12 ❶ 928 51 50 00 ❶ 928 51 50 69
🕐 Slot machines 11.00–16.00; bar & game hall 10.00–04.00; restaurant 19.00–04.00

Clubs & discos
Late-night music and dance venues cluster around the Atlántico strip. Each appeals to its own crowd, though many clubbers drift from one to another. Among top names in this area are **Atomic Revolution**, **Buda** (at the Casino), **Harley Rock Diner and Disco**, **Ibiza**, **Paradise**, **Tequila Bar** and **Tropical**. 🕐 Opening hours are generally 22.00–05.00, with most places remaining fairly quiet before 24.00

Cocktail bars
Catering to a more grown-up crowd, several attractive bars offer snacks and meals in the early evening followed by dancing into the small hours.

Exotic cocktails are the speciality. The longest established, the **Waikiki Beach Club** has a large terrace upstairs and a disco or live music downstairs. ⓐ Centro Comercial Atlántico ⓣ 928 51 24 21 ⓦ www.waikiki-beach-club.com

Pubs & bars

Several big bars with screens and entertainment stay open until late. **O'Donoghues**, one of the popular Irish bars, has music ranging from traditional Irish to current hits, singalongs, drinks specials, and the latest sports events on giant screens. ⓐ Centro Comercial Atlántico ⓦ www.odonoghues-lanzarote.com ⓒ 21.30–04.00. Other bars are on an English or Scottish theme. In the Old Port area **Cervecería San Miguel** has a more Spanish flavour, with music, screens and good food. ⓐ Avenida del Varadero ⓣ 928 51 08 25 ⓒ 10.00–03.00

Shows

Some nightclubs offer shows. Those who aren't easily offended might enjoy the comic performances, especially drag shows, at **Lady Muck** (ⓐ Calle César Manrique), or at one of the resort's most popular venues, **Titti Trollop's Music Hall Tavern** (ⓐ Centro Comercial La Penita ⓐ Avenida de las Playas ⓦ www.musichalltavern.com)

⬤ *A beautiful sunset on the water*

Yaiza

More than once this extraordinary, tranquil little village in the south of Lanzarote has won the contest to find the 'Most Beautiful Village' in Spain. Its simple, traditional white houses, small and unpretentious, form an oasis of light and a stunning contrast to the starkness of the volcanic environment that creeps to its very edges.

In the other direction, away from the volcano that looms so close, the village looks towards the sunburnt farmland that surrounded it completely until 1730. This is when Timanfaya began the six-year eruption that by the end had destroyed half of Yaiza's farms and most of its houses. The villagers first of all fled for their lives, then made their way back to their derelict homes to rebuild what they could.

Today, it is hard to believe that such devastation ever occurred. With dazzling white walls, Yaiza's handsome little houses – sometimes charmingly adorned with balconies or flowers, palm trees or gardens – look well ordered and comfortable. The village became the inspiration for César Manrique, who eventually established architectural rules to help the whole of Lanzarote preserve this simple, traditional appearance.

Inevitably, Yaiza has since become a magnet for visitors. Manrique would not have minded that – he expected it, which is why he restored an old Yaiza farmhouse as a stylish restaurant, La Era, although sadly this is no longer open. On the edge of the village, a couple of traditional old country houses have been turned into smart little hotels of character. Several other village houses have become elegant self-catering accommodation.

Yaiza makes a perfect base for exploring the national park, for visiting Timanfaya before the tour buses have arrived from the other resorts, or after they have departed, and for imbibing the atmosphere of the lonely *malpaís*. It is also well placed for visits to all the other sights of western and southern Lanzarote, and, despite its inland situation, is only a short drive from resorts and sandy beaches such as **Playa Blanca** and **Puerto del Carmen**.

BEACHES

Yaiza is only 15–20 minutes' drive from the sandy beaches of two resorts. **Puerto del Carmen** (see page 57) offers a lively atmosphere and plenty of seafront facilities. Or for a quieter, family setting and a choice of good, sandy beaches with safe bathing, choose **Playa Blanca** (see page 39).

THINGS TO SEE & DO

Camel rides

Yaiza is believed to be the only place in the world with a specially constructed underpass so that camels can cross the road. If you would like to ride one of them in the *malpaís* or up to the top of Timanfaya, call in at the **Echadero de los Camellos** (Camel Park), 3 km (2 miles) north of Yaiza.

ⓐ Parque Nacional de Timanfaya road ⓒ 09.00–16.00

⬥ *Enjoy a camel ride up to the top of Timanfaya*

Village centre

The centre of the village has an arty, civilised atmosphere. There is a municipal art gallery in the **Casa de Cultura** (signposted in the village), while the **Galería Yaiza** art gallery (also signposted) displays local painting and ceramic work, most of which is offered for sale. In the main square, Plaza de los Remedios, step inside the cool 18th-century village church.

Walking

The area around Yaiza is criss-crossed with a network of walking and cycling trails, a legacy of the paths used by farmers and traders of the past. This pretty village is situated at the edge of Timanfaya National Park, surrounded by Lanzarote's ash-black vineyards, and is an ideal base for trekking.

EXCURSIONS
Fuerteventura & Isla de Lobos

Under 20 minutes away, on the fast road across the flatlands south of Yaiza, is the port of **Playa Blanca**, from which ferries and excursions leave several times daily for the neighbouring island of Fuerteventura (see page 93) and the smaller Isla de Lobos (see page 94).

Volcanic landscapes

The volcanic *malpaís* starts at the edge of the village, with the border of the Parque Nacional de Timanfaya just 8 km (5 miles) away. At the heart of the national park, Mount Timanfaya itself, and the coach tour of the **Montañas del Fuego** (Mountains of Fire) that surround it, is a must (see page 82). Only 4 km (2½ miles) from Yaiza (via Uga) are the volcanic vineyards of **La Geria** (see page 76).

TAKING A BREAK

El Campo ££ A good, unpretentious establishment near the village football pitch, this is the locals' top choice for a range of popular local

and international dishes such as fresh fish, meat stew and pizzas.
🅐 Football ground (signposted) 🕿 928 83 03 44 🕒 09.00–23.00

Casona de Yaiza £££ Once voted Best Restaurant in Lanzarote by an
Italian glossy magazine, this small and intimate eatery is part of the

🔺 *El Golfo's spectacular volcanic landscape*

Casona de Yaiza rural hotel, located at the very back of the village facing the Fenauso Valley. The talented chef creates a superb blend of Mediterranean and Canarian dishes using fresh produce. ❸ Calle el Rincón 11 ❶ 928 83 62 62 ❷ 13.30–16.00 & 19.00–23.00 Mon, 19.00–23.00 Tues–Wed & Fri–Sun; closed Thur; closed Jun

AFTER DARK

Beyond a leisurely dinner and a stroll under the stars, there is little nightlife in Yaiza itself. The neighbouring village of **Uga** has a bar with karaoke. For a large selection of late-night bars, pubs and clubs, take a taxi into nearby **Puerto del Carmen** (see page 57).

❶ *Lanzarote's dramatic west coast*

EXCURSIONS
Out & about

Southern tour

There is an intimate, rustic feel to much of the southern half of the island. Despite containing the *malpaís* which consumed so much of their farmland, this remains the Lanzarote of the country people, where their traditions and culture are most accessible. Take the main exit road from Puerto del Carmen, and, on reaching the roundabout at the edge of town, cross straight over to continue via Tías and San Bartolomé towards Mozaga.

THE TOUR

❶ Monumento al Campesino (Monument to the Countryman)

At the junction outside the wine village of Mozaga stands César Manrique's curious sculpture dedicated to the *campesino* – the long-suffering farming man on whose labours, he believed, the whole of society rests. The extraordinary monument, in a cubist form, has been created from an assemblage of discarded fragments of farm and fishing implements, water tanks and fishing boats, and depicts a farmer standing among his animals.

Casa Museo del Campesino (Countryman's House Museum)

Alongside the Campesino Monument is another work by Manrique dedicated to Lanzarote's farming people, the Casa Museo del Campesino. Inside are the rooms of a typical country dwelling of some decades ago, complete with utensils and other equipment, as well as workshops where traditional craftsmen can be seen at their trades. Their products are on sale in the museum's crafts shop, and there is also a good, inexpensive country-style restaurant serving classic local dishes.

ⓘ 928 52 01 36 ⏱ Museum 10.30–17.45; restaurant 13.00–16.00

Mozaga

Straight ahead, Mozaga is an authentic, attractive unspoilt wine village. It has good *bodegas* where you can buy local wines. On the edge of the village, Caserío de Mozaga is a small, chic hotel and restaurant of great

character in a beautifully restored country house that was built at the end of the 18th century.

ⓐ Mozaga 8 ☏ 928 52 00 60 ⓦ www.caseriodemozaga.com
ⓔ reservos@caseriodemozaga.com

❷ Museo Agrícola El Patio (El Patio Agricultural Museum)

Continue from Mozaga to rustic Tiagua, where the Agricultural Museum is a restored traditional farm acting as a vivid record of local life a century ago. Guides take you to see the farm's restored windmills, a cactus garden, fascinating, eclectic displays on local arts, crafts and

⬧ *César Manrique's Monumento al Campesino*

architecture, and a permanent exhibition of old photographs. After the tour, wine tasting is available, and there is a small bar.

ⓐ Echeyde 18, Tiagua ☎ 928 52 91 34 ⓦ www.museoelpatio.com
🕐 10.00–17.30 Mon–Fri; 10.00–14.30 Sat; closed Sun

❸ Ermita de los Dolores (Hermitage of Our Lady of Sorrows)
The Tinguaton road leads across open country and, on the edge of the village of Mancha Blanca, reaches a large church inset with jet-black volcanic stones. This is the Hermitage of Nuestra Señora de los Dolores (Our Lady of Sorrows), the focal point for the island's biggest annual religious celebration, the Festividad de la Virgen de los Volcanes on 15 September, when local people honour the Virgin for saving them from destruction during the volcanic eruption of 1824. There is a simple bar-restaurant opposite the church.

❹ Parque Nacional de Timanfaya
The southwest road begins to cross black and grey volcanic terrain and enters the volcanic area of the Parque Nacional de Timanfaya (see page 79).

❺ El Golfo
Reaching the national highway, bypass Yaiza and take the right turn for El Golfo, on the brutally volcanic west coast. Here the pounding Atlantic has eroded a half-submerged volcanic cone into an exquisite emerald-coloured lagoon amid a backdrop of colour-streaked cliffs.

To go down to the lagoon, look for the small road (signposted) 2 km (1 mile) before El Golfo village, and follow the footpath. The village of El Golfo is acclaimed for its restaurants that prepare excellent fresh fish and shellfish.

❻ Salinas de Janubio (Janubio saltpans)
Some 8 km (5 miles) south along the desolate coast is the lagoon that has become the angular, geometric Janubio saltpans. Salt production has long been an important feature of the island economy, for use in fish preservation.

❼ Yaiza

Continue on the road 8 km (5 miles) back into Yaiza (see page 66). **El Campo** in the village makes a good place for lunch.

❽ Uga

Pretty Uga consists of simple and traditional small white houses. This wine village has plenty of greenery and provides a sharp contrast to the volcanic landscapes that lie nearby. Apart from wine, Uga is known for its camel (dromedary) breeders. **Restaurante Gregorio (££)** is the village inn, serving local specialities. ☏ 928 83 01 08 ⌚ 10.00–23.00; closed Tues

❾ La Geria Valley

Leaving Uga, turn onto the LZ-30 La Geria Valley road, which quickly enters a strange landscape of broken grey *malpaís* where grapes are cultivated. Beside the road – narrow and difficult driving in places – are vine bushes that produce Lanzarote's best crisp white malvasia wine. Each vine bush nestles in its own separate hollow, individually protected by a horseshoe of piled-up lava rocks. As you pass one of the occasional roadside *bodegas*, stop by to taste, and maybe buy, some of the wine they produce. After some 10 km (6 miles) the road passes the oldest *bodega* in the Canaries, **El Grifo**, still a leading name.

❿ Mácher

Retrace your route to the Mácher turning (7.5 km/5 miles from Uga), which leads over a hill to the small community of Mácher, where several upmarket holiday villas look down towards the sea. Continue across the main road back into Puerto del Carmen.

Northern tour

The northern half of the island includes quiet agricultural landscapes that are surprisingly green and gentle in places, with few signs of volcanic presence. Along the way are unspoilt villages and towns, and several unmissable sights. Avoid following this route on a Sunday, the one day when the road may be busy. Leave Arrecife on the main Tahíche and Teguise road.

THE TOUR

❶ Fundación César Manrique

Arriving at Tahíche, note the remarkable César Manrique sculpture standing at the roundabout just before the town. Turn left here to arrive at his former home, now the Fundación César Manrique (see page 83).

❷ Teguise

Passing through pleasant rolling country, and skirting the popular self-catering villa development at Nazaret, the road reaches Teguise, the island's historic former capital (see page 88).

Castillo de Santa Bárbara (Santa Barbara Castle)

On the hill of Guanapay beside Teguise, this handsome fortress of pale stone was first built in the 14th century by Lancelotto Malocello to guard against Arab pirates.

The castle houses the **Museo del Emigrante Canario**, a fascinating museum about the emigration of Canary Islanders to the Americas. After the volcanic eruptions of the 18th and 19th centuries, a large proportion of Lanzarote's population fled to Venezuela.

Reached via a signposted track on the other side of the main road as it bypasses Teguise. ☎ 928 84 50 01 ◷ 10.00–15.00 Mon–Fri, 10.00–14.00 Sat & Sun

❸ Haría

Follow the LZ-10 road as it climbs on the way to Haría. Along the route are some fine viewpoints. A left turn signed to **Ermita de las Nieves** leads

up to a small white chapel with panoramic views. Tranquil Haría, with its picturesque narrow streets and squares, white walls and brightly coloured flowers, stands amid this lush greenery, and is home to around only 2,000 inhabitants. Haría holds a lovely arts and crafts market. ● 10.00–14.00 Sat

❹ Guinate Tropical Park

Continue north on the main road for a further 5 km (3 miles) until it reaches this popular birdlife centre, which has more than 300 species on view and puts on entertaining parrot shows. ⓐ At a right turning, just past the village of Guinate ❶ 928 83 55 00 Ⓦ www.guinatepark.com ● 10.00–17.00

❺ Mirador del Río

The road reaches its most northerly point at the Mirador del Río bar and restaurant. Arguably Lanzarote's loveliest view is from the balcony and panoramic windows of this vantage point. Inside the café, a domed white room cut into the rock looks out over a shimmering turquoise channel called El Río to the little island of La Graciosa. ⓐ 7 km (4$^{1}/_{2}$ miles) north of Haría

❻ Arrieta

The northern road then turns sharply southward towards the southeast coast. Passing the turning to the Cueva de los Verdes (see page 87) and Jameos del Agua (see page 85), the road skirts the village of Arrieta (see page 87).

❼ Jardín de Cactus (Cactus Garden)

On the approach to Guatiza an astounding 8-m (26-ft) cactus comes into view standing beside the road. It turns out to be a metal sculpture, made by César Manrique, and marks the entrance to his Jardín de Cactus. The garden is an amazing display of 10,000 ornamental cacti arranged in descending concentric circles. There is also a snack bar overlooking the gardens (ⓐ Guatiza ❶ 928 52 93 97). Continue on the same road back into Arrecife. ● 10.00–19.00

Timanfaya

It is the hottest spot in Lanzarote. The red-streaked summit of Timanfaya rises from a solidified sea of twisted lava. Every visitor to the island is drawn to its summit. Visible from afar, the volcano dominates the view and the thoughts of visitors and locals alike. Its catastrophic force in an instant once destroyed the livelihood of most of the island, yet now it is Lanzarote's most stunning attraction. There are 36 volcanic cones within the national park, and several others throughout the island, yet Timanfaya is the most awesome.

PARQUE NACIONAL DE TIMANFAYA

It was César Manrique who in 1970 first began the campaign to have the volcanic zone around Timanfaya made into a national park. There were already many visitors to the mountains, and in that year he had opened his volcanic El Diablo restaurant. In 1974 the Parque Nacional de Timanfaya was created. Manrique designed its comical logo, a little devil with horns, tail and trident, conjuring up a sense of fiery mischief.

🔺 *Parque Nacional de Timanfaya*

The park extends beyond the volcanic summits to include part of the area reshaped by lava and debris in the volcanic eruption of 1730.

🅐 All access is on a single public highway that crosses one edge of the park from Yaiza to Mancha Blanca; within the park, a turning leads off the road to a ticket booth and up to the Islote de Hilario. Cars are allowed (free parking), but the usual way to visit the site is on an inclusive bus tour from the resorts. ❶ 928 84 00 57 ⏱ 09.00–17.45

Islote de Hilario

The car park, restaurant and start of the bus tour (see page 82) are at a location called Islote de Hilario, just below the park's highest point. This is where the lingering volcanic heat remains hottest. Ten centimetres (4 in) below the surface, the temperature of the earth reaches around 140°C (280°F); at 6 m (20 ft) deep it is 400°C (750°F); while just 13 m (43 ft) underground the temperature reaches 600°C (1,110°F). Here, wardens entertain visitors by throwing bunches of twigs into hollows where they burst into flame, and pouring buckets of cold water into holes in the ground – the water roars straight back as a jet of steam.

❗ There are free parking facilities at the Islote de Hilario. The coach departs at about hourly intervals throughout the day from 10.00 to 16.00.

🔺 *The volcanic landscape*

THE LATEST ERUPTIONS

The Mountains of Fire are still alive but taking a nap. The Timanfaya eruption of 1730–6 was among the longest and most powerful periods of volcanic activity ever recorded. It devastated the most agriculturally productive part of the island, turning it into a lifeless desert of ash and lava. This was followed by a series of earthquakes culminating in the eruption of the Tinguaton volcano from 1812 to 1824. Both eruptions increased the surface area of the island, pushing the coastline out into the Atlantic. Currently there are no signs of imminent volcanic activity.

VOLCANIC LANZAROTE

All the Canary Islands were formed by volcanic eruptions millions of years ago, and some of the islands remain volcanic to this day. The island most dramatically affected by its volcanic power is Lanzarote. The southern third of the island contains the national park and the large area of *malpaís*, or badlands, around it, but several other parts of the island have similar landscapes, especially the Corona *malpaís* in the northeast.

THE TERRAIN

The Lanzarote *malpaís*, both inside and outside the limits of the Parque Nacional de Timanfaya, contains examples of all the kinds of volcanic material thrown forth by volcanoes: small pyroclasts (ash particles); large pyroclasts (lumps of rock shaped like a rugby ball); *picón* (small solid particles like pebbles); pumice (lightweight fragments of rock, often with razor-sharp edges and shot through with air bubbles); and lava (rope-like formations where liquid rock has set solid). Closer to the summits, the terrain is streaked with colour from minerals. The terrain is not entirely barren: much of it is being covered with tiny coloured lichens, while in places small plants have put down roots.

Montañas del Fuego (Mountains of Fire) bus tour

The park entrance ticket includes the fascinating 14-km (9-mile) Ruta de los Volcanes bus tour of the Montañas del Fuego (Mountains of Fire), the volcanic craters of the Timanfaya eruption. The bus follows a narrow, winding circular route among the peaks, giving views into volcanic cones, across collapsed underground tunnels and over vistas reaching the sea. The tour takes in the **Montaña Rajada** viewpoint, the **Valle de la Tranquilidad** (Valley of Tranquillity), the edge of Timanfaya itself and several smaller craters.

Echadero de los Camellos (Camel Park)

From the foot of Timanfaya, it is possible to travel up the slope of the volcano on the back of a camel. Passengers travel one each side in a wooden seat, the animals being led in a line up the slope. The trip takes about 10 minutes.

ⓐ 3 km (2 miles) north of Yaiza ⓛ 09.00–16.00

Centro de Interpretación de Mancha Blanca
(Mancha Blanca Interpretation Centre)

The cool, peaceful Interpretation Centre is one of the few man-made structures in the park. The small white building makes a startling contrast with the dark landscape. However, most of the centre lies beneath the surface, and contains exhibitions, a library, a bookshop and viewpoints onto the surrounding landscape. The vibrating Eruption Hall mimics the ground movements at the time of the 1730 eruption. No smoking and no noise are allowed at the centre.

ⓐ On the through road at the northern edge of the park
ⓣ 928 84 08 39 ⓛ 09.00–17.00

El Diablo restaurant

At the Islote de Hilario, César Manrique's restaurant and snack bar (**££**) is a circle of glass walls giving superb views over the volcanic scene while visitors enjoy excellent examples of the island's specialities, especially baked meat and bread and salty *papas arrugadas* (see page 98), with

🔺 *Inside the Fundación César Manrique*

local wines. The meat and fish are cooked over a large opening in the ground from which air rises from the volcano at 300°C (570°F) or more.
🅰 Islote de Hilario 📞 928 84 00 57 🕐 12.00–15.30

FUNDACIÓN CÉSAR MANRIQUE

After his death in 1992, the home of Lanzarote's most influential artist, César Manrique, became a museum, and the headquarters of the art foundation that he had established earlier that year. However, in addition to the valuable art collection that Manrique bequeathed to Lanzarote, the house itself is one of the most fascinating sights on the island. The dazzling white walls amid the dark volcanic rock, with sharply contrasting bright flowers and well-chosen cacti, the intricacy and brilliant originality of the dwelling, all together create an unforgettable experience.

The art foundation that César Manrique established was created to promote an understanding of the interaction between art and environment. Its primary purpose today is to disseminate the work

and intellectual legacy of Manrique, as well as to assist the conservation
and sustainable transformation of the natural environment.

🔴 Taro de Tahíche (on road to Teguise), 5 km (3 miles) north of Arrecife
📞 928 84 31 38 📠 928 84 34 63 🔵 www.fcmanrique.org
🟢 fcm@fcmanrique.org 🕐 10.00–18.00 Mon–Sat, 10.00–15.00 Sun
(1 Nov–30 June); 10.00–19.00 (1 July–31 Oct)

Exterior

The visible exterior of the building, inspired by traditional local style,
combines dazzling white with jet black. One of Manrique's huge wind-
driven mobile artworks stands at the entrance.

Manrique had a special interest in mobiles, or wind art, and this
extraordinary example is a huge, complex chaos of colour and
movement. This spectacle is best seen at night, when the mobile and the
house are magically dotted with light. Above the entrance, Manrique has
placed his 'logo' – an interlocked C and M supposed to resemble a devil,
the same image that he used for the national park logo.

The garden

Around the house, a lovely garden has been created between white walls
and black stonework, with tiny steps and terraces. Cacti and other
succulents, ranging from tiny details to immense columns, are artfully
arranged against the walls. It is worthwhile to stop and relax, taking in
the scents and the scenery.

Ground floor

With all-white walls, floors and ceilings, the ground floor of the house
has a wonderful cool serenity, though the mood is sometimes shattered
by tour guides with their groups. The whole of this floor is now a gallery
of artworks from Manrique's private collection. Among them are
abstract and modern works by leading 20th-century artists, including
Tàpies and Miró, with some line drawings by Picasso, and several
of Manrique's own dramatic canvases on the theme of explosive,
volcanic power.

Downstairs rooms

Beneath the beautiful but relatively conventional ground floor is Manrique's underground living area of misshapen rooms and tunnels inside bubbles in the volcanic lava. Five volcanic bubbles have been turned into rooms, each with its own colour scheme and matching specially made furniture. In one, a tree grows up through an opening in the ceiling. Openings in the rock form a narrow black-and-white passageway leading from one room to the next.

Outdoor terrace

Manrique used to entertain his guests in an astonishing downstairs recreational area, where an outdoor dining terrace occupies a *jameo* – a collapsed volcanic bubble open to the sky. In this enclosed space with rock walls but no ceiling are the necessities for preparing and serving a meal, including a barbecue grill, an oven and a dining table, as well as an exquisite bathing pool filled from a flowing waterspout.

On leaving the house and walking towards the exit, visitors can relax on an open terrace with a snack bar and shops located in what was formerly Manrique's garage. On sale are souvenirs, books, clothes and Manrique prints.

JAMEOS DEL AGUA

An interaction of natural wonders with man's ingenuity, the Jameos del Agua (pronounced 'hameos del agwa') is one of the most remarkable sights on the island. It stands amid the dark volcanic terrain near the seashore of the Corona coast, in the north of the island. Originally an underground lake inside a volcanic tunnel in the rock, with a partly collapsed roof, the *jameos* attracted the interest of César Manrique. As one of his first major landscape works, he transformed the site into a delightful subterranean world of water and greenery.
ⓐ Outside Arrieta 🕿 928 84 80 20 🕒 Visits 09.30–19.00; nightclub 19.00–02.00 Tues, Fri & Sat; restaurant 19.30–23.30 Tues, Fri & Sat
❗ From 19.30 suitable clothing required; avoid shorts

> ### WHAT ARE THE *JAMEOS*?
> The volcanic areas of Lanzarote are riddled with underground tunnels formed during an eruption. A *jameo* is a cavity produced when the roof of a volcanic cave collapses. In the Jameos del Agua, between the different *jameos*, you will find a concealed clear lake inhabited by tiny fluorescent white crabs.

The underground section

From the entrance, a narrow spiral staircase descends into the ground, reaching an immense cavern with still, warm air full of the sound of little birds flying around among foliage. A restaurant and nightclub dance floor stand beside a small lake. A walkway leads around the shallow transparent lake, in which resides a species of tiny blind crab that lives only here. At the far end of the lake is a bar with tables on a terrace.

The roofless section

Steps lead from the underground lake into the roofless part of the *jameos*, a cavern below sea level that is fully open to the sky. This, too, is a breathtaking sight. Much of the space has been turned into a clear pool with bright white and blue edging. Beyond the pool, a large cave has been fitted out as an auditorium for concerts and shows.

Casa de los Volcanes (House of Volcanoes)

More steps now climb up the side of the roofless section of the *jameos* to reach ground level again, giving views down into the beautiful open cavern. Overlooking the edge of the *jameos*, the Casa de los Volcanes (House of Volcanoes) is a science museum devoted to volcanology that will interest all age groups.

Corona coast

Although most of northern Lanzarote is fertile and cultivated, the barren northeast coastal area stretching almost from Arrieta to Orzola is the creation of the eruptions of the Corona volcano 5,000 years ago. The Corona *malpaís* is riddled with curious geological rock formations.

THINGS TO SEE & DO

Arrieta
Lying a short distance south of the Corona *malpaís*, unspoilt Arrieta is an appealing village, with its low white houses, fishing boats and a good small beach. There are a couple of plain and simple fish restaurants at the tiny harbour.

🚌 22 km (14 miles) north of Arrecife

Cueva de los Verdes (Greens' Cave)
Reached either from the Arrieta coast road or by turning off the main northern road, the Cueva de los Verdes (the cave once belonged to a family called Verdes) is a spectacular 2-km (1-mile) section of a 7.5-km (5-mile) labyrinth of tunnels. Visitors are taken on an hour-long guided walk through an underground world with lighting and music.

🚌 Near Arrieta, 1 km (½ mile) from Jameos del Agua ☎ 928 84 84 84
🕐 10.00–18.00 (last tour 17.00) ❶ It can be slippery and the tunnel is sometimes narrow

Orzola
Take the coast road that skirts between the dark *malpaís* and the sea. Reaching the northern boundary of the Corona *malpaís*, and near the northern tip of Lanzarote, the road arrives at the handsome little fishing port of Orzola. There are several good, simple fish restaurants facing the water. The harbour is also used by the small ferry to the offshore Isla de la Graciosa (see page 89).

🚌 15 km (9 miles) north of Arrieta

EXCURSIONS

Teguise

Founded in the 1400s, Teguise remained Lanzarote's capital for centuries and acquired several imposing buildings in grand colonial Spanish style. They survive to this day, although Teguise is now just a small and peaceful country town, albeit with an almost African flavour. Every Sunday morning it springs to life as its narrow white cobbled streets and squares are packed with thousands of visitors for the weekly market.

HISTORY

Maciot de Béthencourt, nephew of Lanzarote's legendary Norman conqueror Jean de Béthencourt, chose to build his capital at the very centre of the island, as far as possible from the Arab raiders who constantly attacked from the sea. It remained the capital until 1852, when its port, Arrecife, overtook it in importance.

THINGS TO SEE & DO

Thanks to architecture that is almost opulent by Lanzarote standards, Teguise keeps an aristocratic air. In Plaza de la Constitución, the handsome main square, stands the town's historic principal church, **Iglesia de Nuestra Señora de Guadalupe**. Close by, **Palacio de Spinola** (or Espiñola) is a grand, 18th-century private mansion now preserved as a museum. In the smaller square, Plaza del 18 de Julio, admire the 17th-century **Casa Cuartel**, originally an army barracks, and a 15th-century hospital.

Teguise Market

There is an exotic touch about the Sunday morning arts and crafts market that fills almost every one of the town's narrow lanes. Among the thousands of visitors and stallholders from the other islands there are many who have come over from West Africa, including musicians and entertainers. Local performers sometimes play folk music on traditional Canarian instruments.

🕒 10.00–14.00 Sun

Isla de la Graciosa

The little island of La Graciosa looks its best, perhaps, when seen from the Mirador del Río (see page 78), but for those who take the ferry across the 2 km (1 mile)-wide El Río channel for a closer look, La Graciosa is a delightful place for a day away from it all. Utterly peaceful, it consists predominantly of sand dunes with patches of volcanic terrain, with high volcanic hills in the interior, and a few green areas with vineyards and farms and windmills. For visitors, La Graciosa is a place of activities, leisure and sports, attracting sunbathers, walkers, sport fishermen, surfers and yachtsmen.

The island has two tiny villages, the port of **Caleta del Sebo**, an authentic fishing village where there are two simple restaurants, and

⬥ *A breathtaking panorama of La Graciosa*

Pedro Barba, mainly devoted to summer visitors staying in holiday homes and self-catering accommodation rentals. Both villages are located on the protected El Río channel between the two islands. La Graciosa's total population is 500. No motor vehicles are allowed on the island, so cycling and walking are the norm. With an area of only 4,144 ha (10,240 acres), the island is small enough to walk round in a day.

A day trip to La Graciosa in a modern glass-bottomed catamaran provides an easy, enjoyable way to see the island. The tour run by Líneas Marítimas Romero leaves from Orzola in the morning, with free time at Caleta del Sebo, an excursion to the other smaller islands and the waters of the marine reserve, snacks and lunch on board, and a trip to a beach for swimming and exploring. Bus transfers between Orzola and the resorts are provided.

There is also a regular ferry service. Ferry crossings between La Graciosa and Orzola are operated by **Líneas Marítimas Romero**.
ⓐ Calle García Escámez 11, Caleta del Sebo, Isla de la Graciosa
ⓣ 902 40 16 66 Ⓦ www.lineas-romero.com ⓔ info@lineas-romero.com
ⓛ The Orzola to La Graciosa ferry departs at 10.00, 12.00 & 17.00 (& 13.30, 18.30 in summer). La Graciosa to Orzola: departures at 08.00, 11.00 & 16.00 (& 12.30, 18.00 in summer). The journey takes about 30 minutes each way

THINGS TO SEE & DO

Natural park & marine reserve
In 1985, the whole island of La Graciosa was declared a natural park. Beyond La Graciosa is a cluster of tinier islands, all together forming the Chinijo Archipelago. In 1995, the whole archipelago became the Isla de la Graciosa Marine Reserve, the largest marine reserve in Europe.

An island walk
The ferry arrives at Caleta del Sebo. The only road on the island, little more than a dirt track, leads away from the quayside, northward towards the two volcanic hills in the centre of the island, Mojón and

the twin peaks of Pedro Barba. Another small island, Montaña Clara, can be seen in the distance. Follow the track as it veers right towards the village of Pedro Barba. Turn left before reaching the village to keep walking around the volcanic Pedro Barba peaks, keeping the mountain on your left. Another peak, Montaña Bermeja, rises on the right. Straight ahead is a beautiful coastline of dark rocky outcrops and a long sandy beach, Playa de las Conchas. The island of Alegranza can be seen in the distance.

Before the beach, turn left at an intersection of paths, to take a southward direction back towards Caleta del Sebo. The Mojón volcano is now on the right, the two Pedro Barba crests on the left. There is a good view of the sheer Famara cliffs ahead. The path returns into Caleta del Sebo. The walk takes around four hours. Do remember to wear a hat and take enough water and food, because there is no shade along the route.

⏢ *No motor vehicles are allowed on the tiny Isla de la Graciosa*

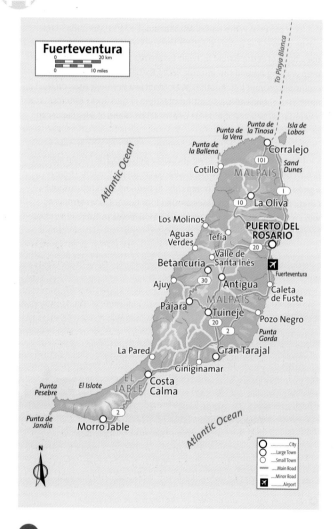

Fuerteventura

0 ——— 20 km
0 ——— 10 miles

To Playa Blanca

Atlantic Ocean

Punta de
la Ballena

Punta de
la Vera

Punta de
la Tinosa

Isla de
Lobos

Corralejo

Cotillo

MALPAÍS

Sand
Dunes

`101`

`10`

La Oliva

`1`

Los Molinos

PUERTO DEL
ROSARIO

Aguas
Verdes

Tefía

Valle de
Santa Inés

`20`

Betancuria

Fuerteventura

Ajuy

`30`

Antigua

Caleta
de Fuste

Pájara

MALPAÍS

Tuineje

Pozo Negro

`20`

Punta
Gorda

`2`

La Pared

Gran Tarajal

Giniginamar

Punta
Pesebre

El Islote

EL
JABLE

Costa
Calma

Punta de
Jandía

`2`

Morro Jable

Atlantic Ocean

N

○ .... City
○ .... Large Town
○ .... Small Town
— .... Main Road
— .... Minor Road
✈ .... Airport

Fuerteventura & Isla de Lobos

A day trip to Fuerteventura is a major attraction. Lanzarote's much larger neighbour is just 25 minutes away on a pleasant sea crossing. For anyone staying in the resort of Playa Blanca, where the regular ferry leaves from, it is too convenient to resist. For others, frequent inclusive excursions are organised by tour operators and local travel agencies. Many inclusive trips also take in a visit to tiny Lobos Island, just off the north coast of Fuerteventura.

FUERTEVENTURA

The closest of the Canaries to Africa, the island of Fuerteventura feels like an offshoot of the Sahara, hot, dry, empty and sandy. The name means 'strong winds', and, although these blow only occasionally, they are sufficiently strong to have brought enough sand to create immense dunes on the east coast. The island is the least populous of all the larger Canaries, and over half the inhabitants live in the small capital town, Puerto del Rosario.

Ferries run regularly between Playa Blanca and Corralejo on Fuerteventura. The trip across the 11-km (7-mile) channel takes about 25 minutes. There are also full-day excursions available, which may include a trip around Isla de Lobos. The main ferry operators are **Fred Olsen** (928 10 01 07 www.fredolsen.es run approximately every two hours) and **Naviera Armas** (902 45 65 00 www.navieraarmas.com run every two hours).

Corralejo town

A busy working harbour and a pleasant, small town with plenty of bars and restaurants, and with some nightlife, this is northern Fuerteventura's main resort. There is a small beach of white sand close to the town centre, but more interesting are the vast golden beaches on the southern edge of town and beyond. There is a tourist office at Paseo Marítimo 2 (928 86 62 35).

Sand dunes

It is worth taking a trip on foot or by taxi to see the extraordinary dunes of pale sand that extend for 10 km (6 miles) along the seashore south from Corralejo, and reach about 3 km (2 miles) inland. This desert zone has the protected status of a national park, the Parque Nacional de las Dunas de Corralejo. For the tourist, the main attraction may be beautiful beaches, but for the scientist the sands are of interest for some unusual plant varieties that can live in such an environment, including the yellow-flowering lotus shrub and the bluebell-like echium.

ISLA DE LOBOS

This unspoilt, uninhabited little island 3 km (2 miles) from Corralejo makes an enjoyable addition to a trip to Fuerteventura. It probably takes its name, 'Island of Seals', from the curious, seal-like shapes of dark volcanic rock emerging from the pale sands of the shore. Remember to bring a hat, drinking water and something to eat, as there is only one paella restaurant on the island.

TAKING A BREAK

Rosie O'Grady's £ Live music nightly, tasty familiar dishes from home and a lively atmosphere make this Irish pub one of the most popular spots in town. ⓐ Calle Pizarro 10, Corralejo ⓣ 928 86 75 63 ⓛ 18.30 till late

La Marquesina ££ Close to the harbour jetty, waterside tables provide an enjoyable view of boats coming and going as you enjoy the fresh fish specialities. ⓐ Muelle Chico, Corralejo ⓣ 928 53 54 35 ⓛ 11.00–23.00

Sotavento ££ A big menu of well-prepared fish and seafood makes this one of the best places to eat in Corralejo. There is a choice of meat dishes, and an inexpensive children's menu as well. ⓐ Avenida Marítima 7, Corralejo ⓣ 928 53 64 17 ⓛ 10.30–16.00 & 19.00–23.00; closed Wed

ⓞ *White-washed houses, Puerto del Carmen*

 LIFESTYLE
Island life

Food & drink

Canarios, like other Spaniards, love to eat out with friends and family, tucking into their food with a robust appetite, sharing noisy, convivial conversation, and letting children run and play around the table (there is no Spanish word for 'bedtime', and parents rarely go out without their children). Only the very smartest places demand any degree of formality. Apart from a light early breakfast of coffee and a pastry, mealtimes tend to be late by north European standards; about 14.00 for lunch and 21.00 for dinner. However, an exception is made for tourists. In the resorts, meals are served at all times of day. It is not unusual to see locals finishing lunch while tourists are beginning their evening meal. Hotel dining rooms often serve dinner at 19.00.

INTERNATIONAL EATING

It would be perfectly possible to spend a fortnight on the island and have nothing but Italian food, for example – and many holidaymakers do just that. With the local population so outnumbered by tourists, restaurants increasingly offer an international dining experience, with a variety of familiar home-from-home dishes such as soups, steak and chips, or omelettes. Chinese, Thai, Indian and most other ethnic styles are also widely available. Popular Spanish dishes such as paella, not part of the Canaries cuisine, make an appearance, too.

LOCAL FOOD

Most visitors to Lanzarote eat little, if any, of the local cooking. Yet Lanzarote has a repertoire of its own of delicious local dishes. These are generally available in the more authentic bars or restaurants. When touring the island, look for restaurants called *típico*, meaning 'local style'. The local cuisine is a blend of three main influences. Most of all, it is Canarian, all the islands sharing a common culinary heritage, but Lanzarote has some of its own individual elements, such as a special fondness for meat stews. Least of all, it is Spanish, but it does share a

few elements with the food of the mainland, such as the tradition of tapas – substantial appetisers that can make a meal in themselves.

Fish

Since most of the coastal resorts were formerly fishing ports, it is not surprising that fish is an island staple. More unexpected is that on Lanzarote fish is traditionally salted and preserved instead of being eaten fresh. Among the most popular local specialities is *pescado a la sal*, fish baked in salt; another is *sancocho*, a thick stew of salted fish and vegetables. Freshly caught fish was traditionally eaten only on the coast, but is now widely available. The most common fish on the menu, *abade*, *cabrilla*, *cherne* and *mero*, are all varieties of sea bass. *Vieja*, parrot fish, and *merluza*, hake, also make a frequent appearance. Fresh fish is usually prepared very simply, grilled or fried, and often served with a spicy *mojo* sauce. Another local dish is *espada*, swordfish. There is plenty of seafood, too, such as *calamares* (deep-fried rings of squid), *pulpo* (octopus) and shellfish, especially *gambas* (prawns).

Meat

Wild game and pork are the favourite foods of Lanzaroteños. Rabbit, *conejo*, is especially well liked and inexpensive, and often appears on menus. *Conejo al salmorejo*, rabbit cooked in a spicy tomato sauce, is a Canarian classic. Another mouth-watering island speciality is roast leg of pork. The most popular way to cook meat is in a hearty, rich, savoury stew together with vegetables and pulses such as chickpeas, lentils or beans. Today, this is the dish par excellence, to eat at leisure with friends and family. Meat stews frequently combine several meats in the same pot, typically rabbit and pork. For a touch of tradition, the soup may be thickened with *gofio* (see page 99).

Meat stews

Puchero is a classic Lanzarote stew, thick and savoury, made with lentils, chickpeas, vegetables and two or more kinds of meat, including pork. Similar is *rancho canario*, though with more vegetables and less meat.

LIFESTYLE

Vegetarians beware – even *potaje* (vegetable soup or stew), or stews
with names like *potaje de berros* (watercress soup), contain meat. For
locals, such a dish served with bread and wine makes a complete meal,
but in restaurants a small portion may be offered as a starter.

Mojo

The most uniquely Canarian phrase on the menu is *con mojo*, 'with *mojo*'.
Grilled or fried fish, roasted meats or boiled vegetables – almost anything,
in fact – may be served *con mojo*. *Mojo* (pronounced 'mo-ho') is the piquant
sauce of the Canary Islands. Based on olive oil, it comes in different
versions, and in good restaurants is more or less spicy according to what it
accompanies. *Mojo* comes in two colours – red and green. Coriander and
parsley make *mojo verde*, green *mojo*, which has a refreshing bite, while
hot chillies are used in the spicier *mojo rojo*, red *mojo*.

Cheeses

Mojo is the perfect accompaniment for fried or grilled goat's cheese,
served as a delicious starter. Cheese plays an important part in the local
diet, and is often eaten as tapas or with a glass of wine. Although
Lanzarote does produce goat's cheeses called *conejero*, the best and most
important cheese is brought over from neighbouring Fuerteventura.
Called *majorero*, this traditional Fuerteventura speciality is a gourmet's
delight, acclaimed throughout Spain. *Majorero* is made of goat's milk
with a dense texture and strong but smooth flavour. Older *majorero* can
be coated with oil and paprika or *gofio* (see opposite).

Vegetables

Lanzarote does not have abundant fruit and vegetables. The exceptions
are *batatas* (sweet potatoes), *cebollas* (onions) and, above all, *papas*
(potatoes). The potatoes are almost invariably eaten as the famous
Canarian speciality *papas arrugadas*, literally 'wrinkly potatoes'.
These are new potatoes boiled in their skins in very salty water, leaving
them with a crunchy coating of salt. Usually served *con mojo*, they are
delicious with meat, fish or cheese, or on their own.

Gofio

It was the *Guanches*, the native Canary Islanders, who invented this rough roasted wholemeal flour. Used as a thickener in stews, or mixed into vegetable dishes, it can also be eaten on its own like a grain for savoury dishes or as a flour baked into sweet puddings.

Desserts

Canarios have a sweet tooth, and may finish a meal with the islanders' traditional dessert, *bienmesabe*, a heavy, syrupy, nutty concoction. It is often served with ice cream. As an alternative, try the chocolate version. *Gofio* desserts are rather stodgy and syrupy, but, if you would like to try one, sample *flan gofio* or *frangollo*. Home-made fig ice cream is a favourite local choice for dessert.

Wines

Many Canarios are likely to order a Spanish beer with their food, but the discerning may choose one of the island's local wines. Unlike other Canary Islands, Lanzarote produces excellent fine wines, crisp, dry and white, made from the malvasia grape. Curiously, the very best come from the least likely terrain, the inhospitable *malpaís* of the La Geria Valley, where the grape bushes have to be protected from sun and wind in order to survive. One of the leading La Geria *bodegas*, or wineries, is the oldest in the Canary Islands: Bodegas El Grifo, founded in 1775 (🕾 928 52 40 36 🌐 www.elgrifo.com 🕐 Museo 10.30–18.00 (10.30–19.00 Aug)). Finish off your meal with a tot of *ron miel*, honey rum. This is made from something truly unique to the Canaries, palm tree sap, gathered on the island of La Gomera.

Menu decoder

These are just some of the dishes you might encounter in one of Lanzarote's *típico* restaurants.

SNACKS/SIDE ORDERS/TAPAS

Aceitunas con mojo Olives with hot sauce

Bocadillo (pronounced '*bocadee-yo*') Filled roll

Chipirones Small squid

Ensalada Salad

Gambas ajillo Garlic prawns

Perrito caliente Hot-dog

Queso Cheese

Tapas Snacks

STARTERS

Potaje Thick soup of vegetables and pulses – may contain added meat

Potaje de berros Watercress soup) – may contain meat

MAIN COURSES

Cabrito Kid (goat)

Caldo de pescado Fish, vegetables and maize meal stew

Conejo al salmorejo Rabbit marinated in hot chilli sauce

Garbanzada Chickpea stew with meat

Lomo Slices of cured pork

Pata de cerdo Roast leg of pork

Pechuga empanada Breaded chicken breast or chicken breast in batter

Puchero Meat and vegetable stew

Ranchos Noodles, beef and chickpeas

Ropa vieja Chickpeas, vegetables and potatoes (although meat can be added)

Sancocho Salted fish (often *cherne*, a kind of sea bass) with potatoes and sweet potatoes

DESSERTS

Arroz con leche Cold rice pudding with cinnamon

Bienmesabe A mix of honey and almonds (delicious poured over ice cream)

Flan Crème caramel
Fruta del tiempo Fresh fruit in season
Helado Ice cream
Truchas Turnovers filled with pumpkin or sweet potato

DRINKS

Agua (pronounced 'ah-whah')
  mineral Mineral water
  con gas/sin gas Fizzy/still
Batido Milkshake
Café Coffee
  con leche Made with milk
  cortado Small white coffee
  descafeinado Decaffeinated
  solo Black
Carajillo Coffee with a bit of condensed milk and a drop of alcohol
Cerveza Beer
Leche Milk
Limonada Lemonade
Naranja Orange
Ron Local rum

Té Tea
Vino Wine
  blanco White
  rosado Rosé
  tinto Red

SPECIALITY DRINKS

Bitter kas Similar to Campari but non-alcoholic
Cocktail Atlántico Rum, dry gin, banana liqueur, blue curaçao, pineapple nectar
Cocktail Canario Rum, banana cream liqueur, orange juice, cointreau, a drop of grenadine
Guindilla Rum-based cherry liqueur
Mora Blackberry liqueur
Ron miel Rum with honey, a local speciality
Sangría Mix of red wine, spirits and fruit juices; can be made with champagne on request

LIFESTYLE

Shopping

MARKETS

If you enjoy wandering around markets, you'll find plenty on Lanzarote. The main draw is probably the weekly Sunday morning market in Teguise, which fills all the streets in the centre of this handsome old town. Many thousands arrive to mingle, relax, stroll, eat and drink, enjoy the buskers and maybe buy something. The goods for sale are souvenirs, toys and hippie-style crafts (few traders are locals). Worth looking for, though, are stallholders with displays of good Spanish lace and embroidery.

Every weekday morning from 06.30 to 12.00, Arrecife, Lanzarote's busy capital, has fish and produce markets in Calle Liebre, where the housewives of the town choose the best ingredients for the family dinner. If you are self-catering, join them. At the fish market, look for the sign *Pescado del Barquillo* – literally little-boat fish – for the freshest catch that has just been brought in by the fishermen.

On Friday evenings from around 18.00, Costa Teguise is worth a visit for its after-dark street market in and around the pedestrianised Plaza Pueblo Marinero. Traders sell their own handmade craftwork in a relaxed atmosphere. The resort of Playa Blanca and the northern country town of Haría both have markets every Saturday morning (between about 10.00 and 14.00). These are relaxed, colourful events where some stallholders sell a little food and fresh produce, but the emphasis is on handmade arts and crafts, souvenirs, linens, clothes and other fabrics, ceramics and knick-knacks.

SOUVENIRS

Lace and embroidery are traditional products that make lovely souvenirs. For better-quality versions you'll have to leave the markets behind. There are many shops selling attractive, elegant fabrics, lacework and embroideries with distinctively Spanish designs. These are not cheap, but represent excellent value for skilful workmanship.

Another enticing purchase are the beautiful ceramics you'll see everywhere. Traditional Spanish glazed pottery, including crockery as well

as tiles and other ceramics, are distinctive and attractive. With the airlines' luggage allowance in mind, look out for smaller items.

If you get interested in the art and ideas of César Manrique, then stylish, well-made T-shirts and other clothes printed with eye-catching Manrique designs or his CM personal logo can be bought at the Fundación César Manrique shop (ⓐ Taro de Tahíche ❶ 928 81 01 38) and at resort branches.

Polished semi-precious stones make unusual, attractive souvenirs or gifts. Look out for the locally gathered green stone called *olivina* (olivine), also known as chrysolite, evening emerald or peridot.

The Canaries are no longer a duty-free region but they still benefit from lower taxes. Numerous shops called *bazares* claim to be selling 'tax-free' goods. They stock a huge array of imported items, but beware – prices are often no lower than in the UK. But shoppers who have done their research can pick up a bargain. Try RT Electronics, at Centro Comercial Jameos Playa, Playa de los Pocillos.

◔ *The popular Sunday market at Teguise*

Children

For children, as for grown-ups, the whole island is full of interest and entertainment. The easy-going, tolerant attitude to children, both in the resorts and in the inland villages, ensures that they, too, have a good holiday. They are almost always welcomed, whether into restaurants, bars or entertainments.

Some of the main sights are rewarding for all the family. Children will be as awed as their parents by the water and fire display on Timanfaya (see page 80). The Fundación César Manrique (see page 83), too, will astonish them – when they see that Manrique lived in five air bubbles under the ground. And the whirring, colourful mobiles that Manrique erected at several road junctions on the island are like giant toys.

TOP ACTIVITIES
Boat excursions
For most children, just to have a trip in a boat is a thrill. The child-orientated pirate cruise is one of the many options on offer at Playa Blanca. Ask representatives for details.

Go-karting
On the main highway near Puerto del Carmen, **Gran Karting Club Lanzarote** has something for (nearly) all ages. There is a junior track for ages 12–16, mini-karts for the over-fives, while children over ten can also try their hand on mini-motorcycles called mini-bikes.
ⓐ Carretera las Playas ❶ 619 75 99 46 Ⓦ www.grankarting.com
🕙 10.00–21.00 winter; 10.00–22.00 summer

Guinate Tropical Park
Way up in the north of the island, give the children a break at this popular, child-friendly birdlife centre, which has more than 300 species on view and puts on entertaining parrot shows.
ⓐ Calle Majadita 14, Guinate ❶ 928 83 55 00 Ⓦ www.guinatepark.com
🕙 10.00–17.00

Museo de Cetáceos de Canarias (Canarian Cetacean Museum)

This fascinating museum is all about the whale and dolphin family.
Visitors find out about the Canary Islands' ocean environment and
become acquainted with these remarkable creatures through images,
sound, full-size replicas and biological exhibits.

ⓐ Edificio Antiguo Varadero, Local 11 ❶ 928 84 95 60 ❶ 928 84 95 61
ⓦ www.museodecetaceos.org ⓔ info@museodecetaceos.org
🕐 10.00–18.00

Parque Aqua Lanza (Aqua Park)

Colourful water slides and flumes, gentle rides for the youngest toddlers,
a bouncy castle and more thrilling options for teenagers.

ⓐ Avenida Club de Golf, Costa Teguise ❶ 928 59 21 28 🕐 10.00–18.00

⬤ *Fun at Parque Aqua Lanza*

LIFESTYLE

Sports & activities

Lanzarote has a well-deserved reputation as a sports island, an ideal place for activities on both land and water. Walking, riding and cycling are readily available. Puerto Calero on the south coast is the sailing resort par excellence, while Famara on the north coast is renowned among windsurfers and paragliders. Lanzarote also has one of the world's leading sports and activities resorts, Club La Santa, on the north coast.

LA SANTA SPORTS
Club La Santa, at La Santa 12 km (7¹/₂ miles) west of Caleta de Famara, is a world-class residential sports resort, with superb equipment and facilities including an Olympic pool. It is the setting for major international sports and athletics events, including the tough Ironman Triathlon. Day visitors are welcome, but residential stays must be booked well in advance, through your local agent. UK agents: **Sports Tours Int**. ⓐ 91 Walkden Road, Walkden, Worsley, Manchester M28 5DQ, UK ⓣ 0161 790 9890 ⓦ www.clublasanta.co.uk ⓔ info@clublasanta.co.uk

CYCLING
Bikes can be hired at all the resorts. As well as easy beachside riding, there are more challenging routes in the interior of the island. Companies like **MegaFun** have a wide variety of bikes and other machines. ⓐ Playa de los Pocillos ⓣ 928 51 28 93 ⓦ www.megafun-lanzarote.com ⓔ info@megafun-lanzarote.com

DIVING
Costa Teguise, Puerto Calero and Playa Blanca have several diving centres. The two top names in Lanzarote diving and scuba are: the long-established **Calipso Diving** (ⓐ Centro Comercial Calipso, Local 3, Avenida de las Islas Canarias, Costa Teguise ⓣ 928 59 08 79 ⓦ www.calipso-diving.com ⓔ calipso@arrakis.es ⓛ 09.00–18.00; closed Sun); and **The Dive Centre** (ⓐ Puerto Calero marina ⓣ 928 51 18 80 ⓦ www.divelanzarote.com ⓔ info@divelanzarote.com).

⬥ *Famara attracts many top surfers*

GOLF

The famous 18-hole **Costa Teguise Golf Club** is considered to be one
of the world's great places to play golf (see page 25), but a new
alternative to this is the **Lanzarote Golf Resort** near Puerto del
Carmen (ⓐ Carretera Puerto del Carmen, Tías ⓣ 928 51 40 50
ⓦ www.lanzarotegolfresort.com).

SAILING

Lanzarote is a great destination for learning to sail. Year-round sunshine,
a mild ocean breeze and accommodating currents provide near-perfect
conditions for 'learning the ropes'. A number of sailing schools, including
Endeavour Sailing (ⓐ Marina Azul, Puerto Calero ⓣ 628 47 84 00
ⓦ www.endeavoursailing.co.uk), provide courses and charters for sailors
of all abilities, from complete beginners to salty sea dogs.

SURFING

Surfing facilities are available at all the resorts. Famara (see page 31), on the north coast, is a leading European surfing resort. Among the surfing outfits based there are Calimasurf, who organise residential surfing camps, and long-established Surf School Lanzarote.

Calimasurf

ⓐ Calle Achique 14, Caleta de Famara ⓣ 626 91 33 69
ⓦ www.calimasurf.com ⓔ info@calimasurf.com ⓛ 10.00–21.00

Surf School Lanzarote

ⓐ Caleta de Famara ⓣ 928 52 86 23 & mobile 686 00 49 09
(09.00–10.00 & 17.00–18.00) ⓦ www.surfschoollanzarote.com

WALKING

Canary Trekking

Lanzarote's network of footpaths is opened up by **Canary Trekking**, based at Costa Teguise, who put together guided walks in all parts of the island.
ⓐ Calle La Laguna 18, Casa 1, Costa Teguise ⓣ 609 53 76 84 (mobile)
ⓦ www.canarytrekking.com

Timanfaya Walks

Properly equipped walkers can join guided tours on two marked paths within the Parque Nacional de Timanfaya. The 3-km (2-mile) **Ruta de Tremesana** takes around two hours, exploring the *malpaís* area close to the camel park north of Yaiza. The tougher 9-km (5$^{1}/_{2}$-mile) **Ruta del Litoral** takes about five hours, exploring the undeveloped volcanic coast on the western edge of the park. To enquire or book, contact the Mancha Blanca Interpretation Centre, on the through road at the northern edge of the park. ⓣ 928 84 08 39 ⓛ 09.00–17.00

WINDSURFING

Windsurfing is available at all the resorts, and is especially recommended at Costa Teguise and Playa de los Pocillos.
Windsurfer Paradise ⓐ Calle La Corvina 8, Costa Teguise ⓣ 928 34 60 22 & 928 59 08 62 ⓦ www.windsurflanzarote.com

Festivals & events

Lanzaroteños love a fiesta as much as anyone in Spain. All the festivals and events that they celebrate with such energy are at heart religious, though with a strong element of music, food and having fun.

CARNIVAL

The highlight of Lanzarote's year is the frenzied celebration of Carnival in February, focused mainly near the waterfronts of Arrecife and Puerto del Carmen. It brings at least a week of street parties and a fantastic costume parade accompanied by whistles and drums. On Ash Wednesday there's a bizarre climax, the 'Entierro de la Sardina', or Burial of the Sardine, in which a beautifully crafted model of a sardine is processed through the streets and finally set fire to.

CORPUS CHRISTI

Taking place in June (sometimes late May), this is a dignified, fascinating Catholic festival enthusiastically celebrated on Lanzarote. While in other parts of Spain, the streets are carpeted with flowers, in Lanzarote's version pavements and squares in Arrecife are decorated with *Alfombras de Sal*, elaborate pictures in brightly coloured dyed sea salt.

FIESTA DE SAN JUAN

Three days of bonfires, parties and traditional events celebrate the summer solstice, from 22 to 24 June, culminating in St John's Day or Midsummer's Day, on the 24th. The centre of celebration is the town of Haría and its 'Valley of 1,000 Palm Trees' in the north of the island.

FIESTA DE NUESTRA SEÑORA DEL CARMEN

The fishing ports and coastal towns pay homage to Our Lady the Virgin of Carmen on 16 July. The main focus is Puerto del Carmen, where a decorated statue of the Virgin heads a big procession through the streets before being taken onto fishing boats in the harbour. The ceremony is to bring good luck to the fishing fleet for the next year.

FIESTA DE SAN GINÉS

The islanders say St Ginés watches over their seafaring tradition and protects their sailors and fishermen. In August, the saint is honoured in grand style in all the island's towns with many days of processions, parades and folk dancing in the streets. The centre of activity is Arrecife's Iglesia de San Ginés, beside El Charco lagoon in the town centre.

FESTIVIDAD DE LA VIRGEN DE LOS VOLCANES

During the volcanic eruption of 1824, the residents of Mancha Blanca and Tinguaton prayed to the Virgin to stop the lava reaching their villages. Their prayers were heard, and the lava came to a halt at the edge of the villages. Today islanders flock to the Hermitage of the Sorrows outside Mancha Blanca on 15 September, where volcanic *malpaís* meets green farmland, to honour the Virgin of the Volcanoes.

CALENDAR OF FIESTAS

5 January	Cabalgata de los Reyes Magos (Three Kings Parade), Teguise
February	Carnival
March/April	Village events all over the island at Easter
15 May	Fiesta de San Isidro, Uga
May/June	Corpus Christi
22 June	Fiesta de San Juan
7 July	Fiesta de San Marcial del Rubicón, Femés
16 July	Fiesta de Nuestra Señora del Carmen
25 August	Fiesta de San Ginés
8 September	Fiesta de Nuestra Señora de Guadalupe, Teguise
	Fiesta de Nuestra Señora de los Remedios, Yaiza
15 September	Festividad de la Virgen de los Volcanes

▶ *Clear signposting on one of Lanzarote's many trails*

PRACTICAL INFORMATION
Tips & advice

Accommodation

Price ratings are based on a double room for one night.
£ = up to €100   **££** = €100–150   **£££** = over €150

ARRECIFE
Arrecife Gran Hotel £££ This luxurious 5-star hotel is in the biggest block on Lanzarote. It has breathtaking views over Playa del Reducto and all the facilities of a hotel of this size – swimming pools, gym, spa and sauna. ⓐ Parque Islas Canarias ① 928 80 00 00
Ⓦ www.arrecifehoteles.com Ⓔ info@arrecifehoteles.com

COSTA TEGUISE
H10 Lanzarote Gardens £ Located just 200 m (220 yds) away from Las Cucharas beach, these clean apartments all come with a balcony, kitchen and living area. ⓐ Avenida de las Islas Canarias ① 928 59 01 00
Ⓦ www.h10hotels.com Ⓔ h10.lanzarote.gardens@h10.es

Hotel Coronas Playa ££ This newly built 4-star hotel is in a prime beachfront setting and does not cater for children under 16, making for a relaxing base within easy reach of Playa Bastian. ⓐ Avenida del Mar 26
① 928 82 66 40 Ⓦ www.coronasplaya.com

FAMARA
Bungalows Playa Famara £ These newly refurbished bungalows are excellent value and cater mostly for the surfers, kite boarders and naturists that come to Famara's beautiful beaches. ⓐ Urbanización Playa Famara ① 928 84 51 32 Ⓦ www.bungalowsplayafamara.com

Finca de las Laderas ££ Set in a 19th-century farmhouse, these two refurbished apartments sit on the edge of the Famara National Park with spectacular views over the Famara cliffs. ⓐ Calle Las Laderas
① 928 52 95 41 Ⓦ www.fincalanzarote.com

PLAYA BLANCA

Hotel Natura Palace ££ Elegant 4-star hotel situated next to Flamingo beach, at the foot of the Red Mountain volcano, an area famous for its moonlike landscape. ⓐ Urbanización Montaña Roja ⓣ 928 51 90 70 ⓦ www.hipotels.com

Iberostar Papagayo £££ This 4-star, all-inclusive resort is set in the cove of Las Coloradas beach and features a beautifully designed pool area and outstanding spa complex. ⓐ Calle Princesa Ico 2, San Marcial del Rubicón ⓣ 928 51 91 11 ⓦ www.iberostar.com

PLAYA DE LOS POCILLOS

Hotel Los Jameos Playa ££ Set in a huge palm plantation, these converted houses are in a fantastically appointed complex right next to the sandy beach. ⓐ Playa de los Pocillos ⓣ 928 51 17 77 ⓦ www.seaside-hotels.com

PUERTO CALERO

Hesperia Lanzarote £££ This 5-star hotel overlooking the exclusive Puerto Calero marina is one of the newest and most luxurious on the island. It boasts fabulous views and a swimming pool on each of its three levels. ⓐ Urbanización Cortijo Viejo ⓣ 828 08 08 00 ⓦ www.hesperia.com/hotels

Iberostar Costa Calero £££ Panoramic views of the marina and Fuerteventura, a fully equipped diving centre and state-of-the-art thalassotherapy centre – this modern hotel certainly fits in with Puerto Calero's swish image. ⓐ Puerto Calero ⓣ 928 84 95 95 ⓦ www.iberostar.com

PUERTO DEL CARMEN

Hotel Los Fariones ££ Sitting only a stone's throw from the shore, this 4-star hotel is in one of the best locations on Lanzarote ⓐ Calle Roque del Este ⓣ 928 51 01 75 ⓦ www.grupofariones.com

Preparing to go

GETTING THERE

By far the easiest and least expensive way to visit Lanzarote is on a package holiday. Inclusive packages, operated by all the major travel companies, leave from all over northern Europe several times weekly. You will find tour operators featuring Lanzarote at Ⓦ www.abta.com

For travellers who already have accommodation in Lanzarote, or wish to book hotels directly, both charter and scheduled airlines sell low-cost direct flights to the island from London and most UK regional airports. Find low-cost flights on Ⓦ www.cheapflights.co.uk. You should also check the travel supplements of the weekend newspapers, such as the *Sunday Telegraph* and the *Sunday Times*. They often carry adverts for inexpensive flights.

Many people are aware that air travel emits CO_2, which contributes to climate change. You may be interested in the possibility of lessening the environmental impact of your flight through the charity Climate Care, which offsets your CO_2 by funding environmental projects around the world. Visit Ⓦ www.jpmorganclimatecare.com

TOURISM AUTHORITY

Spanish National Tourist Offices are to be found around the world and will send out detailed, comprehensive information on all aspects of travel and tourism in the country.

UK office ⓐ 22–23 Manchester Square, London W1U 3PX
ⓣ 020 7486 8077 Ⓦ www.tourspain.co.uk
US office ⓐ 666 Fifth Avenue, 35th Floor, New York, NY 10103
ⓣ +1 212 265 8822 Ⓦ www.spain.info

BEFORE YOU LEAVE

All EU and US citizens are free to travel to Lanzarote. No inoculations or health preparations are needed. It is a good idea to pack a small first-aid kit to carry with you containing plasters, antiseptic cream, travel-sickness pills, insect repellent and/or bite-relief cream, antihistamine tablets,

TRAVEL INSURANCE

Have you got sufficient cover for your holiday? Check that your policy covers you adequately for loss of possessions and valuables, for activities you might want to try – such as scuba diving, horse riding or watersports – and for emergency medical and dental treatment, including flights home if required. The European Health Insurance Card (EHIC) replaces the old E111 form, which enables you to reclaim the costs of some medical treatment incurred while travelling in EU countries. For information and an application form, enquire at the post office or visit ⓦ www.dh.gov.uk/travellers

upset stomach remedies and painkillers. Sun lotion can be more expensive on Lanzarote than in the UK, so it is worth taking a good selection, especially of the higher-factor lotions if you have children with you, and don't forget after-sun cream as well. If you are taking prescription medicines, ensure that you have enough for the duration of your visit, and an extra copy of the information sheet in case of loss, but you may find it impossible to obtain the same medicines on Lanzarote.

ENTRY FORMALITIES

The most important documents you will need are your tickets and your passport. Check well in advance that your passport is up to date and has at least three months left to run (six months is even better). All children, including newborn babies, need their own passport now. It generally takes at least three weeks to process a passport renewal, and longer in the run-up to the summer months. Contact the **Identity & Passport Service** for the latest information on how to renew your passport and the processing times involved. ❶ 0300 222 0000 ⓦ www.ips.gov.uk

You should check the details of your travel tickets well before your departure, ensuring that the timings and dates are correct.

If you are thinking of hiring a car while you are away, you will need to have your UK driving licence with you. If you want more than one driver for the car, the other drivers must have their licences, too.

MONEY

Like mainland Spain and much of Europe, the Canary Islands use the euro. You may need some currency before you go, especially if your flight gets you to your destination at the weekend or late in the day after the banks have closed. Traveller's cheques are the safest way to carry cash because the money will be refunded if the cheques are lost or stolen. To buy traveller's cheques or exchange money at a bank you may need to give up to a week's notice, depending on the quantity of currency you require. You can exchange money at the airport before you depart. Credit cards are widely accepted in the Canaries, but make sure that your credit, charge and debit cards are up to date. Photo ID will always be requested when paying by credit card.

CLIMATE

Daytime temperatures do not vary greatly throughout the year, although there is light rain sometimes. Almost all the rain falls in the winter, but even in the wettest months (December and January) rainfall totals average only 2.7 cm (just over 1 in) per month. However, it can be chilly in the evenings during the winter months, so it is advisable to take something warmer to wear then, such as a shawl or jacket.

BAGGAGE ALLOWANCE

Baggage allowances vary according to the airline, destination and class of travel, but 20 kg (44 lb) per person is the norm for luggage that is carried in the hold (it usually tells you what the weight limit is on your ticket). You are also permitted a single item of cabin baggage weighing no more than 5 kg (11 lb), and measuring no more than 46 by 30 by 23 cm (18 by 12 by 9 in). You may take only one bag on board, but you can carry a coat, too, if necessary. Large items – surfboards, golf clubs, collapsible wheelchairs and pushchairs – are usually charged as extras, and it is a good idea to let the airline know in advance if you want to bring these.

During your stay

AIRPORTS

Lanzarote airport, located 5 km (3 miles) from the capital, Arrecife, handles all the international and domestic flights on the island. Some 5.4 million passengers passed through it in 2008, making it the ninth-busiest airport in Spain.

COMMUNICATIONS
Post offices

Letters and postcards will take approximately 10–14 days to reach mainland Europe. Post offices (*correos*) are open Monday–Friday 09.00–14.00 and Saturday 09.00–13.00. Stamps (*sellos*) for letters and cards to the UK cost 60 céntimos and can usually be bought at shops that sell postcards. Postboxes are yellow. If there are two slots in which to post cards, choose the one marked '*Extranjero*'.

Public telephones

There are many telephone booths dotted around where you can make calls with credit cards or using coins. Please be warned that, if you are using coins, you will need lots of them. Calls can also be made from your hotel room, but this is an expensive option.

TELEPHONING ABROAD

To call an overseas number from the Canaries, dial 00 followed by the country code (UK = 44, Ireland = 353), then the area code (leaving out the initial zero) and the number.

TELEPHONING LANZAROTE

To call Lanzarote from the UK, dial 00 34 then the nine-digit number – there's no need to wait for a dialling tone.

The local operator can be reached by dialling 1003. Telefónica, the main telephone company, has several kiosks in tourist areas where you can make metered calls and then pay an attendant afterwards.

DRESS CODES

Unless you are visiting a casino or a very smart restaurant, there is no need to dress up. Topless sunbathing is allowed anywhere on Lanzarote and there are naturist beaches at Papagayo beach, Janubio beach and Guacimeta beach. There are also some at Famara.

ELECTRICITY

Voltage is 220 V, and two-pin sockets are used – UK appliances will need an adaptor.

EMERGENCIES

WHAT TO DO IN AN EMERGENCY

The number for general emergencies is ☎ 112
For the police ☎ 112 or 091
Ask your rep for advice if you have to attend a police station and take your passport.

The main hospital in Lanzarote is the **Hospital General de Lanzarote**, located in Arrecife. There is also a private hospital in the main resort of Puerto del Carmen.

Clinica Lanzarote
ⓐ Avenida de las Playas 5, 35510 Puerto del Carmen ☎ 928 51 31 71

Consulate
The nearest British Consulate is in Las Palmas on the island of Gran Canaria.
ⓐ Consular Section, Calle Luis Morote 6, 3rd Floor,
Las Palmas de Gran Canaria ☎ 928 26 25 08 & 928 26 26 58
ⓦ http://ukinspain.fco.gov.uk/en

If you are a British national and your passport is lost or stolen while on Lanzarote, you will have to get an emergency replacement passport from the consulate, but first you will need to obtain a police report (*Denuncia*) from the National Police (*Policia Nacional*) in the town where it was lost/stolen. Please note it may be necessary to bring your own translator as not all police stations have this facility. Once you have your police report, take it to the consulate along with four passport-sized photos and a letter of confirmation of identity from your tour operator.

The fee for emergency passports permitting one return trip to the UK is around 70 euros. You may be able to claim some of this cost back via your holiday insurance.

GETTING AROUND

Car hire and driving The police are very kind, understanding and helpful, but they are very firm, so do uphold the law. As in the UK, drinking and driving is severely dealt with. Seat belts are compulsory in the front and the back. Children under 12 must travel in the back of the car. Never park where you should not – yellow lines mean 'do not park here' – since they are very quick to tow you away. They have special vehicles called *gruas*, which take the car to a designated place, normally difficult to find, and of course you have to pay to get it back. Never cross a solid line when on a slip road joining a main road – make sure you wait until you get to the dotted line part before filtering in. Remember to give way to traffic coming from your left when you are on a roundabout, and to go round it anticlockwise. If your car uses unleaded petrol, you need *gasolina sin plomo*.

Rules of the road Remember to drive on the right. Motorists must carry their driving licences, passports and car-hire documents at all times. Failure to do so will result in an automatic on-the-spot fine if you are stopped in one of the frequent road checks.

Roads In general, the road surfaces are good. Road markings are clear, but some of the traffic systems can be confusing when first encountered. Be aware that traffic priorities in these complex traffic systems do not always conform to your expectations; for example,

you might find a stop sign partway around a roundabout or even on a main highway.

Parking Parking meters are usually in built-up or popular areas. Here the parking spaces are marked out in blue. Pay at the meter and display the ticket on the windscreen. Parking in side streets is generally allowed except where the kerbs are painted yellow (or green and white in bus-stop areas). Illegal parking results in the car being towed away.

Useful words for drivers

- *aparcamiento* – parking
- *estacionamiento prohibido* – no parking
- *ceda el paso* – give way to the right and left
- *circunvalación* – ring road

Public transport Current bus timetables are available from tourist offices. A regular and reliable bus service operates on the island. Buses mostly operate directly into and out of the capital, as on the spokes of a wheel. This means a change of bus is often necessary to reach a particular destination. It pays to be on the early side, since buses sometimes run marginally ahead of schedule. Not all services operate on Sunday. The Canarian word for bus, *guagua*, is pronounced 'wah-wah'. The main resorts are connected to the capital, Arrecife, with a frequent bus service, mostly half-hourly.

Taxis Licensed taxis are easily recognised by the sign on the roof. Next to the sign is a light that shows green when the taxi is free. Generally, short journeys within towns are not expensive, especially with four people sharing. The taxis are colour coded according to the district in which they operate. For longer journeys outside towns, you should agree a price beforehand.

Ferries & hydrofoils A complex network of inter-island ferries and hydrofoils links the seven main islands of the Canaries, and schedules change very regularly, so you need to check times locally. Most of the inter-island services are operated by **Trasmediterranea** (Ⓦ www.trasmediterranea.es) or the **Fred Olsen Line** (timetable details and online booking at Ⓦ www.fredolsen.es).

Domestic flights The local airline, **Binter Canarias**, provides regular flights between the islands. 📞 902 39 13 92 🌐 www.bintercanarias.com

HEALTH, SAFETY & CRIME
Food & drink precautions Mains water is perfectly safe, but you may not like the taste due to the high volcanic mineral content. Buy bottled water for general drinking, tea, coffee, etc. It's best to buy bottled water from the supermarkets. There are two types available: *agua con gas* is sparkling mineral water and the more common *agua sin gas* is still water.

> **Beaches** In summer, many beaches have lifeguards and a flag safety system. Other beaches may be safe for swimming, but there are unlikely to be lifeguards or life-saving amenities available. It is important to bear in mind that the strong winds that develop in the hotter months can quickly change what appears to be a safe beach into a not-so-safe one, and some can have strong currents the further out that you go.
>
> ## BEACH SAFETY
> A flag system is used to warn bathers when sea conditions are unsafe for swimming.
> - Red flag = dangerous – no swimming, even if other people are doing so. Freak waves may drag you off promenades or rocks.
> - Yellow = good swimmers only; apply caution.
> - Green = safe bathing conditions for all.

Health care Standards of medical care are high on Lanzarote. Although EU residents are entitled to some reciprocal health care in the Canaries, travellers are advised to carry an EHIC (see page 115), which entitles them to medical treatment in any medium-sized state clinic or hospital. Please note that most hospitals and clinics on Lanzarote are private. Make sure you have adequate medical insurance before you travel; all the island

hospitals will accept British insurance and they all have English-speaking staff. A *farmacia* (chemist) can be recognised by a large green cross on a white background. Most of these keep shop hours, but there is always a 24-hour rota system for emergencies. The nearest *farmacia de guardia* (duty chemist) will be listed on the door. At night, only prescription medicines are dispensed.

Crime prevention Take as much care of your personal property as you would at home. Watch out for pickpockets, especially in crowded marketplaces. Crime with violence is unusual, but do not take risks. Leave nothing of value in a parked car, not even locked in the boot. Bag snatchers are around, too, so carry your valuables in a bag securely anchored to your body.

Police There are two security forces on Lanzarote, the local police (*Policía Local*) and the civil guard (*Guardia Civil*). The *Policía Local* have blue uniforms and blue markings on their cars, while the colour of the *Guardia Civil*'s uniforms and car markings is green. If you have a problem – say, with lost or stolen property – talk to your holiday representative or hotel desk; they can help you make an official statement to the police.

MEDIA
English-speaking visitors will not feel cut off from home on Lanzarote. There are a plethora of newspapers and magazines catering for the expat community – and of course the main papers from the UK (at a price). Power FM and Gold FM are the two big English radio stations and satellite television is widely available.

OPENING HOURS
Banks are generally open Monday to Friday 08.30–14.00 and on Saturday 09.00–13.00 in winter only. Shops and businesses are generally open Monday to Friday 09.00–13.00 and 16.00–20.00, and Saturday 09.00–13.00. Within large resorts these hours are often extended and some shops may even open on a Sunday.

Most chemists (*farmacias*) observe the same opening hours as shops. However, there is always a duty chemist (*farmacia de guardia*) open until late and during siesta time in every area. For details of the duty chemist, check in any chemist's window. For travellers staying in the south of the island there is a 24-hour chemist open every day of the year just opposite the Veronicas nightlife area in Playa de las Americas.

Restaurants in tourist areas generally open from 13.00 until late. In quieter areas they may close after lunch at around 16.00 and reopen at 19.30 or 20.00. The Canarian people rarely eat before 21.00 and restaurants are less crowded before that time.

Most museums open only in the morning – usually between 09.00 and 14.00. Museums are usually free on Sundays.

RELIGION

On Lanzarote, as in mainland Spain, the main religion is Catholicism, and almost all the towns and cities, including tourist resorts, have churches where Mass is frequently held.

TIME DIFFERENCES

There is no difference between Lanzarote and the UK at any time. New York is five hours behind, San Francisco is eight hours behind. Sydney is ten hours ahead.

TIPPING

Many restaurants include a service charge in the bill, and so there is no need to tip unless you have received exceptionally good service and wish to show your appreciation. If service is not included, an average tip is considered to be 10 per cent of the bill. This applies to services, taxis and restaurants.

TOILETS

Public toilets are generally found around the beach areas in the tourist resorts. Usually there will be a charge for use of these facilities.

TRAVELLERS WITH DISABILITIES

Most of the main tourist areas have adapted their pavements to enable wheelchair access: Costa Teguise and Playa Blanca are two of the best resorts. However, very few hotels have specially adapted rooms and facilities. If in doubt whether the accommodation or resort you would like to book is suitable, please check with your tour operator.

An excellent online information service for travellers with disabilities within Europe is **Europe For All** ( www.europeforall.com).

The two companies on the island that hire mobility scooters or wheelchairs are:

Island Mobility SL 928 34 95 33 www.islandmobility.com
Mobility Aids Lanzarote 928 34 60 05
www.mobilityaids-lanzarote.com

The island government's webpage also has useful information on beaches and accessibility issues. www.portalturismoaccesible.org

ACKNOWLEDGEMENTS

The publishers would like to thank the following for providing their copyright photographs for this book:

Alamy pages 9 & 74 (Isifi Image Service s.r.o.), 83 (Profimedia.CZ s.r.o.); BigStockPhoto pages 80, 91, 107; César J Palacios pages 44, 69, 89, 111; Dreamstime/Eyewave page 30; Flickr/Mario Menti page 105; Getty Images pages 10–11, 49; Photoshot/World Pictures pages 55, 57, 79; Pictures Colour Library page 33; SuperStock page 103; Thomas Cook pages 1, 5, 13, 16, 20, 24, 37, 42, 52, 60, 65, 67, 71, 95.

Project editor: Catherine Burch
Layout: Julie Crane
Proofreader: Karolin Thomas
Indexer: Marie Lorimer

Send your thoughts to
books@thomascook.com

- Found a beach bar, peaceful stretch of sand or must-see sight that we don't feature?

- Like to tip us off about any information that needs a little updating?

- Want to tell us what you love about this handy, little guidebook and more importantly how we can make it even handier?

Then here's your chance to tell all! Send us ideas, discoveries and recommendations today and then look out for your valuable input in the next edition of this title.

Email to the above address or write to:
pocket guides Series Editor, Thomas Cook Publishing, PO Box 227, Coningsby Road, Peterborough PE3 8SB, UK.

Useful phrases

English	Spanish	Approx pronunciation
BASICS		
Yes	Sí	*Si*
No	No	*Noh*
Please	Por favor	*Por fabor*
Thank you	Gracias	*Grathias*
Hello	Hola	*Ola*
Goodbye	Adiós	*Adios*
Excuse me	Disculpe	*Diskoolpeh*
Sorry	Perdón	*Pairdohn*
That's okay	De acuerdo	*Dey acwerdo*
I don't speak Spanish	No hablo español	*Noh ablo espanyol*
Do you speak English?	¿Habla usted inglés?	*¿Abla oosteth eengless?*
Good morning	Buenos días	*Bwenos dee-as*
Good afternoon	Buenas tardes	*Bwenas tarrdess*
Good evening	Buenas noches	*Bwenas notchess*
Goodnight	Buenas noches	*Bwenas notchess*
My name is ...	Me llamo ...	*Meh yiamo ...*
NUMBERS		
One	Uno	*Oono*
Two	Dos	*Dos*
Three	Tres	*Tres*
Four	Cuatro	*Cwatro*
Five	Cinco	*Thinco*
Six	Seis	*Seys*
Seven	Siete	*Seeyetey*
Eight	Ocho	*Ocho*
Nine	Nueve	*Nwebeyh*
Ten	Diez	*Deeyeth*
Twenty	Veinte	*Beintey*
Fifty	Cincuenta	*Thincwenta*
One hundred	Cien	*Thien*
SIGNS & NOTICES		
Airport	Aeropuerto	*Aehropwerto*
Rail station	Estación de trenes	*Estathion de trenes*
Platform	Vía	*Via*
Smoking/	Fumadores/	*Foomadoores/*
non-smoking	No fumadores	*No foomadores*
Toilets	Servicios	*Serbitheeos*
Ladies/Gentlemen	Señoras/Caballeros	*Senyoras/Kabayeros*